MW00413028

West Academic Publishing's Law School Advisory Board

JESSE H. CHOPER
Professor of Law and Dean Emeritus,
University of California, Berkeley

JOSHUA DRESSLER
Distinguished University Professor, Frank R. Strong Chair in Law
Michael E. Moritz College of Law, The Ohio State University

YALE KAMISAR
Professor of Law Emeritus, University of San Diego
Professor of Law Emeritus, University of Michigan

MARY KAY KANE
Professor of Law, Chancellor and Dean Emeritus,
University of California, Hastings College of the Law

LARRY D. KRAMER
President, William and Flora Hewlett Foundation

JONATHAN R. MACEY
Professor of Law, Yale Law School

ARTHUR R. MILLER
University Professor, New York University
Formerly Bruce Bromley Professor of Law, Harvard University

GRANT S. NELSON
Professor of Law Emeritus, Pepperdine University
Professor of Law Emeritus, University of California, Los Angeles

A. BENJAMIN SPENCER
Professor of Law,
University of Virginia School of Law

JAMES J. WHITE
Robert A. Sullivan Professor of Law Emeritus,
University of Michigan

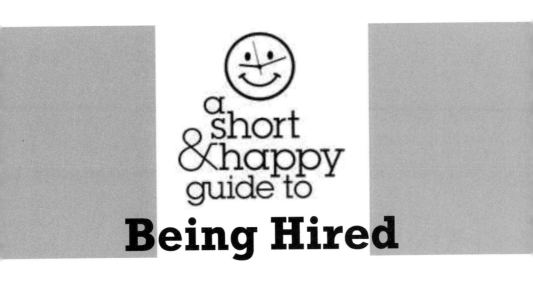

Being Hired

Desiree Jaeger-Fine, Esq.

A SHORT & HAPPY GUIDE® SERIES

WEST
ACADEMIC
PUBLISHING

The publisher is not engaged in rendering legal or other professional advice, and this publication is not a substitute for the advice of an attorney. If you require legal or other expert advice, you should seek the services of a competent attorney or other professional.

a short & happy guide series is a trademark registered in the U.S. Patent and Trademark Office.

© 2018 LEG, Inc. d/b/a West Academic

    444 Cedar Street, Suite 700
    St. Paul, MN 55101
    1-877-888-1330

Printed in the United States of America

ISBN: 978-1-68328-982-1

Table of Contents

A Short & Happy Guide to Being Hired

Before We Start

By the end of this book you will not have reached your job journey's end; you will not even reach the beginning of its end; but you will have ended its beginning.

Thank you for picking up this book. I encourage you to read this book from beginning to end. You may be tempted to look only at the resume or informational interview section, but it is important to understand the foundation upon which a successful job search is built. You can have a wonderful resume and cover letter and yet be unsuccessful in your attempt to secure employment. It is the foundational work that will make the difference in the long run and those that embrace these concepts will succeed.

Likewise, simply reading this book to its last page does not mean that you will receive a job offer. To paraphrase Winston Churchill, by the end of this book you will not have reached your job journey's end; you will not even reach the beginning of its end; but you will have ended its beginning. The end of the book is the beginning of your journey. My words alone will not change a thing, but your actions can and will.

Before we get started, I would like to make a few editorial notes:

- I will use the pronoun "she."

- I will only use "law firm" to make reading easier but most references are equally applicable to other legal employers.

- If I mention a website, *e.g.*, a job board, it may be that the site is taken down between my writing and your reading. That is the pace of the Internet age. It does not affect the value of the information provided, however. The context in which a website is mentioned will stay current.

This book will outline some thoughts that will challenge your current world view and I encourage you to keep an open mind.

And finally, benefiting from this book requires you to subscribe to the idea that hard work can and will lead to success.

It has to start somewhere.

It has to start sometime.

What better place than here?

What better place than now?

Let us get started.

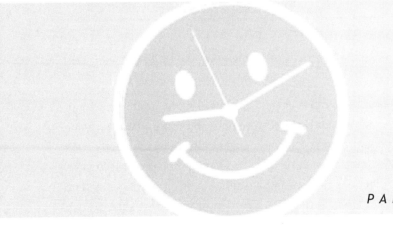

PART 1

Let's Get Started

Survival of the Fittest

Every morning in the wild, a gazelle awakens. One thing is sure for the gazelle that day, as every other . . . She must run faster than the fastest lion. If she cannot, she will be killed and eaten. Every morning, a lion awakens. For the lion too, one thing is certain . . . This day and every day, he must run faster than the slowest gazelle. Whether fate names you a gazelle or a lion is of no consequence. It is enough to know that with the rising of the sun, you better be running, for the rest of your days . . .

—Unknown[1]

Welcome to the world of job hunting. The basics of job hunting seem straightforward: you find an open position, prepare your cover letter and resume, and let your qualifications and education speak for themselves. But experience teaches that job hunting is akin to a chess game—not in that it is complex, but in that it is not the person with the greatest assets that wins, but the person who uses her assets most skillfully. She is the fittest. I see it time and time again: the most successful job seeker is not necessarily the one with the most impressive resume, but the one who understands the game and

3

knows how to play it, the one who knows how to do the necessary things right.

It might surprise you to hear that successful job hunting is less about having the most impressive credentials and more about knowing what to do and then consistently doing those things correctly. One of the most frustrating parts of a job search is delayed gratification and the rejections that we must face. In light of rejections and no noticeable progress in the right direction, it is very difficult to keep doing what we are supposed to do. But just like the gazelle and the lion, with each passing day of our job search, we must run.

This also requires consistent improvement. Rest assured that there are many professionals who consistently progress and dedicate themselves to their improvement. These professionals are not satisfied with being average, they seek to be above average. And this leads to an unavoidable truth: if a whole lot of people are trying to be better than average, they will eventually become the average. They raised the bar. This means that those who do not improve, will eventually decline below average. This is the survival of the fittest.

Know Which Strings to Pull

To succeed in our job search, we do not need special talents. We do not need to be outstandingly skillful, but we need to be a respectable professional. This should be common sense, yet this basic idea is violated by so many job seekers. It baffles me how the easiest things are the ones most often neglected. Just to give you an example: I was asked by a job seeker to review her resume. I offered to do so, and the job seeker took one month to send me the draft. After she sent the draft, she followed up after two days to ask whether I could look at the resume quickly since she had to send it to a recruiter. It took her one month to send it to me and then she requested a return within two days. I, of course, did my best and reviewed the draft while traveling through the Negev Desert.

To this day, two months later, I have not received any reply to my comments on her resume. No acknowledgment whatsoever, let alone a thank you. We don't need a degree in rocket science to understand what is wrong with this behavior. If a search for a candidate with her credentials comes my way, she will not be one of my recommendations. Not because I mean to be spiteful, but because I can't. Her behavior will reflect on my judgment as to what a good candidate is.

Like this job seeker, many sabotage their job searches and careers with behaviors that can easily be altered. Our job application is not comprised of just a cover letter, resume, and transcript. It is our entire professional persona and that in turn is a window into who we are as a professional and future employee. We can spend many chapters on drafting a perfect resume. But our job search will not get anywhere if we focus just on a perfect resume. A successful job search has multiple components, each of which needs to be perfectly aligned. As the captain of this endeavor, we need to have a comprehensive understanding of all the constituents and how to navigate them in the most effective way. It is quite common for candidates to succeed who may not look so strong on paper but have a perfect sense which strings to pull and when. Working efficiently, Peter Drucker explains, means knowing how to do things the right way, but working effectively means doing the right things.

Familiarity Does Not Equal Knowledge

It is easy to confuse familiarity with knowledge. Many things that we will discuss are familiar to you, but this does not mean that you have reached the level of knowledge required to properly execute them. You have heard about resume and cover letter objectives many times before, but that does not mean that your resume accomplishes what it is supposed to. When you read this book, try to read it with an open and fresh mind. Try not to skim over parts just because you feel that you have heard it before.

Simplicity Does Not Minimize Importance

Many things that we will discuss will cause a "Duhhh" reaction. But it is the "Duhhh" things that will make the difference. Difficulty is not always proportionate to importance. Just because something seems obvious does not make it less important. Just because something seems easy to implement does not make it less important. It is the little things that make a big difference. The one who underestimates the little things is the one without the job offer.

Goal Focus Alone Will Not Assist Us

Our end goal is a job and every day and with every undertaking we will be thinking about this goal. We have heard it before: goals are important. But goal setting that takes our focus away from the process is detrimental. If we loath the process, we will never go anywhere. I have never heard a job seeker being obsessed with perfecting the process. The process—working, improving, and consistently hitting incremental targets—is what will make us a winner. Like rock climbers, if they are focused on the top, and if they are looking up, they are going to fall. Instead, their focus is, "Where am I going to put this hand next?" "Where am I going to put my other hand?" Where am I going to put this foot?" "And where the other foot?" Each move is a destination and they are very much engaged in the process itself. Focus on the process and perfect execution of each and every step.

Short & Happy

- The person who will win is not always the person with the most assets but the person who uses her assets most skillfully.

- Working efficiently means knowing how to do things the right way but working effectively means doing the right things.

- Do not confuse familiarity with knowledge. Always be ready to learn something new in what you have heard before.

- Difficulty is not always proportionate to importance. In job hunting, it is the simple things that will make the difference.

- Be obsessed with the process and focus on its perfection. The goal can be reached only by perfecting incremental steps.

Failure

Life is not about how hard you hit, it's about
how hard you can get hit and keep moving.

—Rocky Balboa

At some point in our lives we will be job hunting unless we are independently rich. Whether we seek our first job, whether we seek to transition into another field, or whether we are forced to seek a new position by circumstances outside of our control, we will all face the same difficulties. Things do not get easier later in life, nor does the strategy change in any meaningful way.

And one thing is for certain, no matter when or why you are job hunting, you will fail along the way. Failure is not only part of our job hunt, it is an essential part. Applications will remain unanswered and interviews will not be successful. If we want to avoid failure, we will have to do nothing. And is this not the ultimate failure? We will be rejected, and our applications will be ignored. But in the pursuit of our dream job, who cares how many times we are rejected? The result is what matters.

But we must deal with failure, not just ignore it. Dealing is active, ignoring is passive. We should extract information contained in that failure so that we can improve our pursuit. If a failure is converted into improvement, it is net positive. Only failure that leads to counterproductive feelings like frustration is bad. If we use failure as a tool to improve, however, we will get closer to our goal with each failure.

Nothing in this book is intended to avoid failure. Before you read on you should think about how you will deal with the inevitable failure that you will meet. What are your strategies for improvement? How will you channel your frustration and disappointment? How will you remain steadfast in your confidence and stay positive amidst rejection?

Know that failure is coming, embrace it, extract necessary information to improve, and move on.

Short & Happy

- Failure is an inevitable part of your job search. Learn to deal with it.

- Do not ignore failure but deal with it by extracting information that helps you improve in your pursuit.

The Loser's Game

Rather the pain of discipline than the pain of regret.

—Bob Andrews

"Strategy is a route to achieving your objectives," says Simon Ramo. Mr. Ramo has an impressive record of achieving his objectives. At 72 he is a world-renowned scientist and engineer. He was the chief architect of America's intercontinental ballistic missile system and is the "R" in TRW, the multi-billion-dollar industrial conglomerate. Ramo's current objective is very down to earth—he wants to win more often at tennis. After years of playing "merely ordinary" tennis on the court at his estate in Beverly Hills, he decided that it was time to improve his game strategy.

Ramo identified the crucial difference between games played by amateurs and those played by professionals in his book "Extraordinary Tennis for the Ordinary Tennis Player." According to Ramo, professional players win a game by scoring more points against their opponents. This is called a Winner's Game. Amateur players, on the other hand, do not beat their opponents by scoring points, but lose the game by conceding points. In other words, professionals win against other professional opponents by superior skill, while amateurs lose against their amateur opponents by making more mistakes. This scenario is called a Loser's Game.

Amateurs lose not only by making more mistakes, but also by taking more chances against other amateurs in an effort to win. This over eagerness causes them to make even more errors. While a player's victory in one circumstance is determined by the skill of the professional, victory in the other is determined by the mistakes of the amateur.

Under which category does the job search fall? Is it a Winner's or a Loser's Game?

A Loser's Game encompasses situations in which the competition is fierce and of equal ability. Being able to win such a Loser's Game would require a substantial edge, which most people will not be able to accomplish or demonstrate in such a strongly competitive environment. There is no doubt that in this legal market the competition is fierce and the abilities, especially those of junior associates, are somewhat equal. The job hunt is a crystal-clear Loser's Game.

Where does this leave us? Our strategy of winning, of succeeding, therefore, is to avoid making mistakes. The example of the woman whose resume I reviewed and who had not written a thank you note is a perfect example of beating oneself by mistakes. In the meantime, I wrote to her to ask whether she received my resume and I was greeted with silence. She has no sense of basic professionalism and this will make her pursuit of a new job very difficult.

We must also avoid trying too hard. If we do not master the basics we will never achieve excellence. If we elevator pitch up the wazoo at a cocktail reception, without having understood basic principles of professionalism, then the mistakes we make will cause us to lose the game. Let us stop focusing on being better than others and instead focus on playing an error-free game.

This goes against everything we believe to be the case. Many job seekers try to build a superior personal brand, try desperately to score, while neglecting to master the basics and avoiding mistakes. Mistakes in our foundational work will sabotage our success. I am not saying that we should never strive for outstanding achievement. The point is that we can only do so once we have mastered the basics.

The job seeker with a solid foundation making the fewest mistakes will win the game. Much of what determines a successful job hunt is persistently solid performance rather than outlandish superiority.

Doing good, mistake free work consistently rather than a one-off stroke of genius is what matters. Sounds too easy to be true? Mastering foundational skills is by no means easy. Just ask athletes who painstakingly practice basic moves a thousand times.

Mistakes Versus Failure

In our second section we talked about failure. Failure is not to be confused with mistakes. Failure is an outcome; a mistake is a cause. We can have a solid foundation, perfect applications, and amazing interviews, and still be declined for jobs because of things outside our control. This "failure" is unavoidable and part of the game. What we must do is analyze whether it was based on our mistake and whether there was something that we could have done better.

Short & Happy

- The job search is a Loser's Game.

- Job seekers do not beat the market by scoring points, but you may beat yourself by making mistakes and conceding points.

- Focus on consistent, mistake-free performance.

The State of Confusion

> If there is no struggle, there is no progress.
>
> —Frederick Douglass

Confusion is the most common state of mind I find my job seeking clients in. Confusion about the situation, confusion about what to do next, and confusion about why what they have done so far has not worked out. We are also often confused as to our role in the job search process. We understand that we have to apply for a job, but what else can we do? What, if any, are our other responsibilities? We feel that we are at the mercy of the market, that we must patiently sit until a position opens, is then posted on job boards, and our application answered with an invitation to an interview. When others tell us that we must do more we are confused about what they mean by "more." We cannot apply more if there are no more job postings. How can we possibly influence the market, the availability of a position, and the employer's opinion? Does this not seem utterly out of our control?

Confusion is also a result of an overload of options that we are lucky enough to be facing. We may feel like we do not have any options, but we do. The problem is not being optionless, the problem is navigating the sea of options. It is much easier to say yes to an offer after our summer at a firm than to decide whether we want to work at a firm, an NGO, or a company.

Being confused is not a concern. Not doing anything about it is. Confusion reflects a lack of information, and we can remedy that. While some will let confusion paralyze them until they resign and believe that their fate is out of their hands, others will actively seek information that clarifies the situation and enables them. The only way out of confusion is to inform ourselves until we are in a position to act. We need to be able to find information that clarifies the situation and our role in it. Most importantly, we need to find information on what exactly we can do to take the job search into our hands and be less dependent on luck.

Seeking new information is only the first step. We also have to carefully watch our attitude towards that new information. If our view of the situation is that we are at the mercy of the market and that important factors are out of our control, we may seek information that confirms that belief. Moreover, faced with new information that contradicts what we believe, we may change the meaning of the new data to fit our old view of reality. The interpretation of information can vary among people significantly. If information contradicts how we perceive the situation, we have to be open to accept the validity of the new information and be willing to adjust our behavior accordingly.

Information is the way out of confusion and the responsibility for seeking it is ours. But no matter how much information we gather, there will always remain a modicum of confusion. There is no three-step route to a new job. Every path is different and rarely are the paths straight. Many paths to success twist and turn and we will find ourselves confused quite frequently. Being confused does not mean we have to sit at home waiting for enlightenment to strike us. We must be out there and plow the field. Read, ask, listen, seek, analyze, move, act. If we start that process early, we can approach our job search from a position of clarity and control. If we wait too long, and the situation becomes dire, our focus becomes centered on escaping from a toxic situation rather than moving toward an opportunity.

Short & Happy

- Confusion reflects a lack of information.

- Find information that clarifies the situation and do not rest until you find it.

- Watch your attitude toward new information. If information contradicts how you perceive the situation, be open and accept the validity of the new information and adjust your behavior accordingly.

Response-Ability

It is not enough that we do our best; sometimes
we must do what is required.

—Winston Churchill

Are you willing to take responsibility for the outcome of your job search? You are quick to answer "of course." But do you truly feel responsible? Have you ever caught yourself thinking "a law degree is not worth what it was in the past" or "the law school career services office is not doing its job properly" or "bar associations should offer more of this and that" or "people don't understand that I don't have time to network but need to find a job now"? Responsibility can be abdicated but it cannot be delegated. You can give it up, but you cannot pass it along—not to the law school career staff, your mentors, or anyone else in your network. If you do not take responsibility, no one else will.

Responsibility is not to be confused with blame, which implies that someone is at fault for a negative situation. No one is blaming you for not having found a job. But everyone is asking you to take ownership of the process.

Responsibility is positive and empowering. It is a "response-ability": the ability to choose our response in every moment to all that is going on around us. This allows us to claim ownership of our career, and thereby, to contribute to making it better. Saying that someone is responsible is a positive statement, contrary to how many perceive it. If I tell you that you are responsible for your job search, you may be offended, you may think that I am heartless. But what I am trying to do is to empower you. We should, therefore, not only accept responsibility but embrace it.

Taking responsibility for our job search means that we do not waste energy on complaining about things that are outside of our control. Taking responsibility also means that we are comfortable considering our potential role in a problem. We are inclined to seek the roots for a problem outside of us. But a responsible person will first look at herself. If we distance ourselves from our potential role in a problem, we also distance ourselves from the possibility of our place in the solution.[2]

Short & Happy

- Responsibility can be abdicated but it cannot be delegated.

- Be comfortable considering your potential role in a problem. If you distance yourself from your potential role in a problem, you also distance yourself from your place in the solution.

- Responsibility is positive and empowering and not to be confused with blame.

Laser Focus

In addition to accepting and embracing responsibility we need to have a laser sharp focus on our objective. In German, there is a saying that can be translated as "someone is like a banner in the wind." This describes someone who does not have a strong core and whose actions are influenced constantly by outside forces. In a conversation with a client I can tell fast how focused that person is. You can see it in the language used, in diversion, and in facial expressions. Being focused on our objective does not mean that we are closed to receiving input and advice. It means that whatever comes our way is assessed in light of our objective and evaluated for its effectiveness towards achieving it. Do not be a banner in the wind; decide on what you want to achieve and work towards making it happen.

The focus on an objective and taking responsibility go hand in hand. If I ask a job seeker about her objectives I often hear "I am not sure" or "What do you think?" It does not matter what I think, the job seeker is the only person who can and should attempt to answer that question. We are empowered to answer it and we are responsible for doing so.

We are afraid to decide on an objective for two reasons. We fear that it may be the wrong decision and we think that being open to anything exposes us to more opportunities. Both assumptions are wrong. Let us first look at the fear of making a wrong decision. It does not matter whether our answer is the right one in the end. What matters is that we decide. Indecision is the root of many problems. Nothing is set in stone and we can always change our minds. How can deciding on a possible wrong decision still be favorable than not deciding at all? Because indecision is disabling. If we decide on a goal, we start acting. If we stay in limbo, we remain inactive. Being passive and inactive is the worst situation a job seeker can find herself in.

Moreover, an objective clarifies our actions. If we are active without an objective, we will just be hopping around like a crazy person. An objective allows us to evaluate an action as to its efficiency in reaching our objective. We are much more selective. We act, and we act more effectively.

Let us now look at the argument that being open to anything equals more opportunities. We will discuss this in more detail in the second part of the book but for now consider this: have you ever decided on buying a certain car or a certain piece of jewelry, let us say a blue Mercedes or a Cartier watch, and noticed something afterwards? No matter the object, the minute you have decided on that object you start to see it everywhere. Did Cartier watches suddenly multiply? Obviously not. The only difference is that you are now tuned into seeing them. How can you find something in this sea of information and options without knowing what you are looking for? Once you focus on a goal you are far more likely to see information that helps move you towards that objective. Being open-minded is a good thing, but it does not exclude deciding. You can be both, an open-minded decision maker.

Before you begin your job search, answer these important questions:

What do you want to do next?

What is important to you in your next job?

What law firms could use your specific talents and expertise?

Take responsibility, decide on an objective and stay focused.

Short & Happy

- Indecision is disabling. Decide!!

- It does not matter whether your decision is the right one in the end. What matters is that you decide.

- Being open to anything does not lead to more opportunities, it only blinds us to see what is right in front of us.

- Decide on a blue Mercedes today and you will see them everywhere.

The "Job Search in a Bubble" Syndrome

Nobody said that it would be easy; they just
promised it would be worth it.

—Anonymous

Intelligence Is Power

Since the beginning of time, the role of intelligence has been vital to human survival. Knowing where your enemy is, what he is doing and planning, and what he is capable of has always been crucial. Almost every country has an intelligence agency: a government agency responsible for the collection, analysis, and exploitation of information in support of law enforcement and national security. I am not comparing our job search with war. We do not even have an enemy, besides ourselves. But there is something important regarding intelligence gathering in war and national security that applies equally to our job search: the importance of information. The job seeker with the most information who also knows how to use it will succeed faster than the one with less information or with information that she does not know how to use.

It is astonishing how little job seekers know about the legal market in which they seek to spend a big chunk of their lives. It is particularly astonishing considering that we find ourselves in a day and age where searching for information is what we do day in and day out. I did not count how many times I used my phone today to look up some sort of information, but I know that it was many times. We are a generation of skilled Internet users and search the web every day. Yet when it comes to our job search we sit in a bubble. How can this be? To make this neglect even more striking, let us remember that we are lawyers who pride ourselves on our research skills. In our job search, however, we do not research in any meaningful way. Of course, the average job seeker researches a law firm by looking at its website prior to an interview. If she is slightly above average, she may have had an informational interview or looked at the website not just before the interview but before sending the application. But this research has nothing to do with the intelligence gathering that is required to efficiently navigate the legal market.

When job seekers sit in my office and say that they do not know what to do it is almost always due to lack of information. We cannot know what to do if we have no clue what is going on around us. We need information to decide. We need information to act. Therefore, one of the most important elements of a successful job search is the skill of collecting, analyzing, and exploiting information. The diffusion of information is a crucial aspect in our job search. Mark Granovetter brings it to the point in his study on contacts and careers by saying that "[t]he actual transmission of information about job opportunities becomes a more immediate condition of mobility than any characteristic of jobs themselves."[3]

This was not covered during your last career boot camp? What was surely covered though was the necessity to research the employer. This is usually discussed with regards to interview preparation. This is a very limited application of the need to gather information and utterly too late in the process. I am not saying it is wrong. I am saying it is too late and not enough. If my job search is based on valuable information I will not have to hastily look at the firm's website the evening before my interview. I can sleep peacefully because I know why I am going to interview at that place in that moment in time and that I am a great fit because otherwise I would not have even wasted my time with it. We ended up with this interview purposefully and not by happy accident.

The ease of access to information is a remarkable feature of our generation. There has never been a time before where so much information was at our fingertips 24/7. How can we neglect using it in our job search?

From Data to Information to Knowledge

Some job seekers collect data, but data does not equal information. Data is raw unorganized facts that needs to be processed, organized, and structured and its significance determined. Once it is organized in a useful manner it becomes information. If the information is then connected to a purpose—to our objective—it becomes knowledge. It is a skill we need to acquire and the better we are at it, the more successful we will be not only in our job search but also in our career.

Many job seekers go online and print a list of law firms. They have done their research and now have information, so they think. They then come to me and tell me that they are unsure about how to proceed with this list. They are unsure because they stopped at the first step—they produced data. They now must go further and process this data—the raw list of law firms. Are all firms relevant? Where are they located? What practice areas do they have? What size are the firms? etc. Only once the list is organized and structured and the significance of its features determined will we produce information. But we are still not done. We, finally, need to connect that information with our objectives to achieve knowledge about the proper course of action.

At this point we must be very careful. It is here where we should not get caught up in our end goal, the goal of finding a job, as mentioned before. Focusing on our end goal might lead us to send our resume to the hiring partner or human resources manager of every law firm on the list, which is not effective as you may already have experienced. Instead, we must focus on taking incremental steps and perfecting the process. Such an incremental step would, for example, be a conversation with a junior attorney to learn more about the firm's current climate, culture, etc. That information may in turn help us to set up an informational interview with a partner. Before you act, decide what it is you want to accomplish next— receive a piece of information, make a connection, or have a conversation, for example. Focus on incremental steps; your next step is rarely a job offer.

Our primary role as a job seeker is to be an investigator, a collector of information. Like a detective, we should look for clues. To be the best at it we need to be an astute observer and listener, willing to connect the dots and act upon valuable information. Collect data, process and organize it to receive information, connect the information with your objectives, and gain knowledge to a proper course of action. She who knows how to use information will get that job offer.

Not All Information Is Valuable

The value of information depends very much on how many people have access to it. Information about an available position that is posted online and, thereby, accessible by thousands of applicants is less valuable than information about an available position coming from a trusted colleague prior to its posting. The same is true for information on a firm's website. Job seekers look at these websites to inform themselves, but the truly valuable information will only come through people who work there. The more people that have access to the same information, the less valuable it becomes.

How to Find Information

The first question is: how do you know what information to look for? Well, this depends a lot on where you want to end up. Not knowing what to search for is a reflection of not knowing what we want to find. If I were to say to you "Find me something on the Internet" you would instantly ask me "What are you looking for?" It is impossible to search for just anything.

The second question then is: how do you know where to look for it? The answer is: the market. And as any market is comprised of goods and services provided by people, why don't we start with people? Simply talk to people! The job seeker is usually frustrated with that answer. What they really want to hear from me is that there is a secret platform with a database that only a few have access to, sort of like the Freemasons for job seekers. If that does not exist, which it doesn't, then they hope for a secret 1,2,3 guide that is distributed only to a select few. Again, there is no such thing. The job search is a fairly easy process if one is willing to eat the broccoli. Information is power. She who has the most information is enabled to act the best and the fastest. Information is in the market and the people working in it can share more than any other information outlet.

Let me give you one example of a situation in which job seekers lack sufficient information. How can we conduct a proper job search if we do not know how the other side's mechanisms are working? When I say that we should not be in a bubble, I include knowledge about the employer's search for talent. I am astonished by how little job seekers know about what is happening on the employer's side. Hiring is an extremely expensive, time consuming, and frustrating endeavor for any employer. It is not only the job seeker who worries about the job search, the employer does too. How to find the right employee may seem simple considering the supply. But finding the right candidate is more complicated than we may imagine. Just do a quick Google search on advice for recruiters and HR and you will find many "how-to" guides for every part of the employee search process. Questions such as "How do we plan our hire and what is our budget? What do we write in the job ad? How and where do we post the job? How will we collect applications? How do we progress candidates from applied to hired? Should we work with external recruiters? Who should be on the hiring team? How many steps does a candidate go through prior to a final interview? Do we conduct background checks prior to a final offer?" are just a few of the many issues employers have to tackle. As job seekers we rarely consider recruitment software, forests of resumes and bottomless email threads, giant spreadsheets, and a constant wrestling match to coordinate interviews and feedback. If we are unfamiliar with the hiring process, we cannot properly position ourselves to be the beacon of light the employer is looking for.

I quite often receive the question "Can I pay you to do this for me?" What would this look like? Consider again that the bulk of information comes through people. And people only share information with those they trust, and they trust those they have a relationship with. What do you think happens if I introduce a total stranger into the mix? How is she going to benefit from the relationship that people build with me? She would have to start all over building a relationship of trust.

Short & Happy

- Information is power. The transmission of information about job opportunities is more important than any characteristic of jobs themselves.

- Be an investigator—a collector and processor of information.

- Information is in the market and the people working in it can share more than any other information outlet.

- Do not dismiss information that contradicts your belief about a situation—embrace it and adapt.

- The more people who have access to the same information, the less valuable it becomes.

- Move from data to information to knowledge.

The Active Versus Passive Job Seeker

> Some people want it to happen, some wish it
> would happen, others make it happen.
>
> —Michael Jordan

There are two types of job seekers: the active and the passive. The passive job seeker visits job boards, sends applications, and has a few conversations here and there. This sounds quite active to you? Running in a circle is an activity as well, but not a very productive one. Centering one's job search around job boards is passive because we are merely reacting to other people's actions. We are dependent on their action, posting a job, without which we cannot re-act. This is not a good position to be in. Reactive people wait for things to happen to them, but they never make things happen.

The active job seeker, on the other hand, is constantly seeking new information about the law firms she is interested in and the people that work there and leverages information to make an informed decision on how to act next, *e.g.*, who to contact, how, and what to ask. By actively scouring the market rather than waiting for firms to post openings, the active job seeker is one step ahead of the competition.

By being one step ahead of the competition we simultaneously limit the competition. We will find roles before others, before information about the job availability is advertised and its value, therefore, diminished. Instead of competing against an entire army of job seekers we may be one of a few. That puts the odds very much in our favor.

By moving away from the passivity of a job board centered job search approach, we will also avoid frustration, as you may have already experienced. Scouring job boards and applying for positions is frustrating. That frustration may turn into doubt and desperation. We start to internalize the lack of responses from employers and begin to believe that something must be wrong with us or our resume. It is not an issue with us but with what we do or do not do.

Action Requires Energy

Have you ever seen an energetic job seeker? That is a rare species. With every passing hour energy is sucked out of them and they become more, and more reactive. Energy is the cornerstone of life. We cannot be active without energy. An energetic and active job seeker beats a passive one every time. We must have a high amount of energy during this process. The less energetic we are, the less likely we are to receive a job offer.

Action Requires Excitement

Have you ever seen an excited job seeker? That is a rare species, as well. Why not be excited about the potential to change our future? The potential for a great and satisfying job? This is a tremendous journey you are embarking on.

An energetic, excited, and active job seeker is difficult to find. If you show energy and excitement throughout the process, you will stand out.

Short & Happy

- Reactive people wait for things to happen to them, but they never make things happen.
- Move away from the job board centered job search approach.
- An energetic and active job seeker beats a passive job seeker every time.
- Be excited about the opportunity to create your future.

The "But" Person

The other day I was at my Olympic weightlifting class and the drill was to slam the hip against a 33-pound bar hard enough to make the bar audibly vibrate. It hurt like hell and after the 10th time my hip was red and sore. I made the mistake of replying to the coach's request to try harder with "It hurts." He said, "I don't f$%&ing care." I was stunned not by his remark but by my mine. Here I was trying to improve my lift while complaining about the pain involved in the process. I was fixed on the goal of being able to lift without committing myself fully to the painful process of getting there. My coach was right, he should not care. If I want to improve my lift, I will have to deal with the pain. So, I shut up and slammed my hip against the bar.

Job seekers consistently complain about how uncomfortable the job search is. If they want to find a job, and a job they like, they will have to embrace the process.

If you want to achieve something, it will hurt. No one will or should care about your discomfort. This is true in athletics as it is in the legal market. Your pain is irrelevant. It is irrelevant because it is part of the process. It is required to achieve something and everyone else had to go through it before you. Everyone! Do not make the mistake of thinking that you are the only one struggling.

No Excuses

There is not a single excuse that we can come up with that someone would consider valid. Not a single excuse. With every seemingly benign excuse, we make ourselves less marketable. People do not care about our pain, but they care about our excuses. Excuses make us look ridiculous. The most ridiculous excuse a job seeker can use is that they do not have time. If you do not have the time to make your job search your priority, do not expect others to make it their emergency. Excuses communicate only one thing: incompetence; in this case the incompetence of time management and professionalism. How can a job seeker think that she is busier than a partner for M&A for the Americas at a major U.S. based law firm? The former takes two weeks to answer an email, the latter four minutes. This is a real-life example. It just makes me want to pull my hair out. While the former is busy making excuses, someone else is getting hired. Do not seek other people's compassion, seek their respect.

Scratch the following sentences from your vocabulary: "I don't have the time," "I couldn't find. . .," "No one not told me that. . .," "I found out too late. . .," I couldn't make the deadline because. . .," "My family came to visit. . .," "I had a bad cold. . . ."

Stop Making Excuses!

At this point you might think "But, Desiree. . . ." Allow me to interrupt you right here. The job seeker who uses the word "but" is the one without a job. The frequency of the use of "but" is proportionate to one's failure in achieving success. The word "but" is a word without value. If someone gives you advice, a suggestion or a recommendation, no "but" in the world will be of assistance to you. If someone asks me for advice and she replies with "but. . .," I know that I will not be able to help her. It is impossible to help a "but" person. A "but" person is someone who seeks others to validate their preconceptions. They use the word "but" to start an excuse for their shortcomings. They are not interested in learning or improving. They seek someone to feel pity for them. Scratch the word "but" from your vocabulary.

Short & Happy

- If you do not have the time to make your job search your priority, do not expect others to make it their emergency.

- Excuses communicate only one thing: incompetence.

- With every seemingly benign excuse, you make yourself less marketable. Stop making excuses!

- Do not seek other people's compassion, seek their respect.

- The frequency of the use of "but" is proportionate to one's failure in achieving success.

- Don't be a "but" person—a person who seeks others to validate their preconceptions.

---

1   https://quoteinvestigator.com/2011/08/05/lion-gazelle/#return-note-2567-2

2   https://www.psychologytoday.com/blog/finding-your-voice/201311/accepting-responsibility

3   Granovetter, Mark. *Getting a Job: A Study of Contacts and Careers.* Second Edition. Chicago, IL: University of Chicago Press, 1995 at 6.

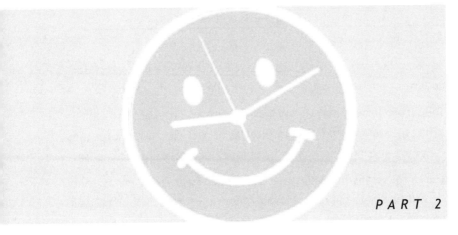

PART 2

What to Search for

Two Roads to Nowhere: Anything and Nothing

It won't happen overnight, but if you
give up, it won't happen at all.

On December 6, I received the following email in reply to my question "What type of position are you looking for?":

Dear Desiree, concerning what I want to do, I am open to anything and everything that allows me to use and build upon my . . . skills.

What if we were to meet and I would ask you to "Find me anything and everything." You would likely stare at me a bit puzzled and be concerned about my well-being. Yet, job seekers take pride in their search for anything. Their argument goes something like this: I am in no position to be picky and should be open to any opportunity given to me.

There are three issues with the "anything approach." The first issue is that many job seekers use the "anything approach" to avoid addressing what they need to address: what do you want to do in your career? Introspection is neglected among most job seekers. If I

29

do not know what to search for I have two options: I can search for nothing or anything. Both lead to the same place: nowhere.

The second issue is that if they know what to do, they are not willing to put the work in that is required to achieve it. So, they opt for the "anything version." "Anything" seems so much easier to accomplish.

The third issue is the belief that being open to anything means that we will find more opportunities. In other words, that choosing a goal limits opportunities.

None of this is true. The search for anything is an outcome of indecision. Deciding takes courage.

The willingness to accept any job offer must strictly be separated from the search object. "Anything" is not a search object. You cannot search for anything. Did you ever search for "anything" on Google? I am sure you never did. You always searched for something. You may have altered your search term, but you did so to find something particular. When you search for a job you must start somewhere and starting with anything will lead you nowhere.

Deciding on a search object is different from our willingness to accept an opportunity that does not align one hundred percent with what we were looking for. The decision to choose an opportunity that was not intended has nothing to do with our search object. You may be willing to *take* any opportunity, but you should not *search* for any.

It is important to keep these two concepts apart. Never resign yourself to search for "anything." This reflects laziness, of not being willing to decide an important question: what is it that you are looking for?

The most common approach is to apply for a job and then figure out if it is something you want to do. This is as efficient as playing the lottery and then figuring out what we want to do with our life. Until you hit the lottery, you wander around like a banner in the wind.

Most importantly, while you are looking for "anything," an employer is certainly not looking for "anyone." She will be looking for someone whose objective is to work for her and who was willing to put in the required effort to land in her office. If you are looking for anything, you will never be an employer's someone.

When others recommend that we have an elevator pitch we tend to focus on the pitch, on how to make it sound interesting to others. But the most important element of the elevator pitch is that developing one requires that you first decide on what it is you want to do in your career. The elevator pitch is nothing other than the communication of our objectives. Before we can communicate it, we must know what it is. A person who knows what she wants is attractive. An "anything" person is one of many and not distinguishable from the crowd.

Short & Happy

- When you search for a job you must start somewhere and starting with anything will lead you nowhere.

- The search for "anything" is an outcome of indecisiveness.

- Your search object must be differentiated from your willingness to take advantage of a given opportunity. You may be willing to *take* any opportunity, but you should not *search* for any.

- You may be looking for anything, but an employer is not looking for anyone.

- If you are looking for anything, you will never be an employer's someone.

Opportunity Versus Opportunity

As we have said, job seekers often argue that if they are open to anything, they will have more opportunities. This is not so. This idea stems from a misunderstanding of what an opportunity is. Not every available legal position is an opportunity. An opportunity is a situation favorable for the attainment of one's goal and has an apparent probability of success. For a situation to be considered an opportunity a variety of criteria must be met. What does this look like?

Let us assume that you are looking for an entry-level position as a corporate attorney in a mid-size law firm. You are a member of the corporate law committee at the xyz bar association where you frequently attend meetings. You and some of your fellow members organize a program on careers in corporate law during which you get to know each other better. You frequently communicate via email, meet for coffee, and have conference calls. One of those members just heard from a friend that he is looking for a junior attorney for his mid-size corporate practice. He immediately thinks of you and asks whether you would be interested in a conversation. You, of course, send your resume and set up a meeting.

This is an opportunity. The job matches what you are looking for. You match what the firm is looking for and on top of all, you come with a recommendation from a friend.

Now let us change the situation slightly and assume that you find that same position on a job board. You are still the right candidate for the job but the odds in your favor shrink drastically for two reasons. First, your competition is likely expanded by the hundreds. Second, you are missing the highly valuable recommendation. I would still classify this an opportunity, however, with limited odds.

Let us change the situation again and say that you have been looking for weeks now online but no one seems to be looking for an entry-level attorney in corporate law. You change to the "anything approach" and start applying for positions that require a few years of experience, for positions asking for admission in states in which you are not admitted, for some banking and finance positions, some arbitration positions, and even some real estate positions. Basically anything. You then come to me and say "Desiree, I have sent hundreds of applications, but nothing is working out. What is wrong with me?" There is nothing wrong with you but with what you do. You are not applying for opportunities. You are gambling, filling out lottery tickets in the hope that one wins. You hope that one application sticks. None of the positions can be considered to be a situation favorable for the attainment of your goal. There is no apparent probability of success.

Let us look at this from a different perspective. If you invest $10 in bonds you have a real opportunity to get some return on your investment. If you spend $10 on a slot machine in Vegas, you have almost none. What do you want to do with your time and energy? Invest it in bonds or gamble in Vegas?

Recognizing Meaningful Opportunities

One of the skills job seekers need to acquire, therefore, is the ability to analyze a situation and determine whether it represents a real opportunity—a situation favorable for the attainment of one's goal. Our goal is to work so effectively that our actions create real opportunities upon which we can act. To incorporate our discussion on information, our actions should look something like this:

Step 1.   Gather data.

Step 2.   Process that data to produce information.

Step 3.   Combine that information with purpose to acquire knowledge about your next steps.

Step 4.   Act upon knowledge to identify or create real opportunities.

Step 5.   Spend energy only on real opportunities.

Short & Happy

- An opportunity is a situation favorable for the attainment of your goal and has an apparent probability of success.

- Not every open position is an opportunity and worth pursuing.

- Acquire the ability to analyze a given situation to determine whether it represents a real opportunity.

- Only pursue real opportunities.

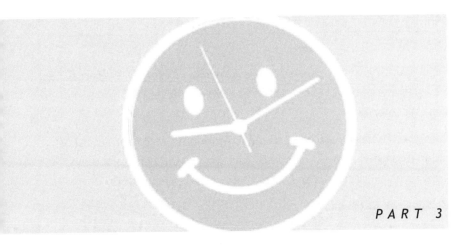

PART 3

Where to Search

Job Boards

The terms job boards and job search engines are often used interchangeably but there is a difference between them and it can be confusing. The main difference lies in the source of the jobs that are listed. There is nothing wrong with using either as long as they are not the foundation of our search. No job seeker's search should depend on job boards or engines. They should make up the smallest piece of the puzzle.

The Good

Job Boards

Job boards are websites which post jobs supplied by employers or recruiters. Online job boards help hiring authorities source candidates for open positions and job seekers find employment. Law firms and recruiters advertise open positions and accept applications directly through these boards. There are both general and niche job boards available. Niche job boards focus on specialized candidates for particular industries. For example, the legal industry would have sites like LawJobs. Other niche boards cater to a segment of the job market like entry-level jobs, summer jobs, or internships.

Employers typically pay a fee to the provider of the job board to list their jobs on the site. Candidates can also upload and store their resume on these boards and make them visible to employers.

Job Search Engines

Job search engines scour the web and aggregate job listings from job boards and employer websites. Indeed and SimplyHired are two of the most popular job search engines and they collect millions of listings on their platforms. LinkUp searches through the websites of small, medium and large employers without including input from job boards. Niche job search engines focus on a particular area. For example, I run a job search engine that focuses on positions for international attorneys.

Job Boards Versus Job Search Engines

Since job search engines contain listings from multiple sources we will find a wider variety of job postings there. However, this is not always better. Please keep in mind our discussion on opportunity and the search for anything. You will have to look through many duplicate listings and a listing does not always mean that a job vacancy is still available or represents a genuine opportunity for you. This sucks up a lot of our time and may be a source of frustration.

The Bad

If we find an opportunity through a job board, we may have to register on that site and some even require a fee to join. We may also deal with a lot of spam and advertisements.

The Ugly

Here is the real issue with job boards. As a job seeker we can pay LinkedIn, for example, a fee of about $30 per month for a "Job Seeker Premium" membership so that, when we apply for jobs, we can artificially move our application to the top of the list as a featured applicant. The employer, on the other hand, will see a flag beside our name suggesting that we paid for the position in that ranking. Neither the job seeker nor the employer can turn this feature off. A hiring employer can pay LinkedIn, as well. A fee of about $3,000 will give the employer 10 job postings to help find the best, most qualified hires. And here is the twist. Would you as an employer not care that those at the very top of the list you see paid LinkedIn for their positioning while possibly better, more qualified candidates who did not pay are pushed to the bottom? Nick Corcodilos in his article "Is LinkedIn Cheating Employers and Job Seekers Alike?" said that the artificial placement of resumes on top of a list for a fee does not serve either the job seeker or the employer but only the balance sheet of the middle man, the job board.

Imagine a headhunter who would charge the employer to fill a job and the applicant to submit her resume first. That is called double-dipping and is frowned upon. It is no secret that once a job is filled, a job board like LinkedIn loses two sources of revenue: the employer and the job seeker. So a successful business model requires that everyone keeps searching. Job board revenues go up when employers and job hunters keep returning to post and search, and when both pay to play.[1]

To Use or Not to Use Job Boards?

Having laid out the good, the bad, and the ugly, where does this leave us? Nothing I said is to suggest avoiding job boards altogether. Our takeaway is to not rely on them exclusively. Use job boards and engines but limit your dependence on them and limit the time spent on them. We will consider how to do this in Part 4 of this book. Below is a list of job boards/engines for you to look at and determine for yourself which seem useful. I am not endorsing any of these, I merely state them.

Select List of Job Boards:

Abalcc.org

Avovethelaw.com/jobs

Bcgsearch.com

Careerbuilder.com

Emplawyernet.com

Findlaw.com

Gobiglaw.com

Goinhouse.com

Indeed.com

Lawcrossing.com

Lawjobs.com

Lawmatch.com

Legalstaff.com

Linkup.com

Linkedin.com

Martindale.com

Monster.com

Nalp.org/jobs

Simplyhired.com

Simplylawjobs.com

USAjobs.gov

Uscourts.gov/careers

Short & Happy

- Job boards are websites that post jobs supplied by employers or recruiters; job search engines scour the web and aggregate job listings from job boards and employer websites.

- A job board dependent job search is an ineffective job search.

- You can use job boards as one resource, but you should limit the time you spend and your reliance on these resources.

Recruiters

Many job seekers are confused about how hiring works, and, specifically, about the role of recruiters. It is important to understand the role of recruiters and how the process works to be effective in our dealings with them.

There are several types of recruiters, but the mechanics of recruiting remain the same. Internal recruiters are employed by a firm for the purpose of finding new talent. As employees, they are paid a salary by that employer. External recruiters are individuals or firms subcontracted by a law firm for the same purpose. External recruiters are also paid by the firm that retained them, but rather than a salary, they are contingency recruiters who are paid a fee only if the firm hires a candidate discovered through the recruiter's efforts. Job seekers often ask about recruiters and the complaints are always the same: "I have sent hundreds of resumes to recruiters, but I never hear from them, and can't get them to return my calls."

It all boils down to this: recruiters are not working for us, the job seeker, but for the hiring firm. It is the firm that pays recruiter fees and they only get paid if they deliver the right candidate. It is the firm, their client, who they ultimately must satisfy. Recruiters do not earn money by helping the job seeker find employment.

Recruiters are typically compensated 20-30%, or more, of the annual salary of each attorney they place. That is a chunk of money. If a firm pays this kind of money they do not wish to be bombarded with resumes of unqualified candidates. A recruiter's reputation depends on how efficiently and effectively she can satisfy the firm's needs. Recruiters will never pass along our resume to help us out. They will only do so if we fit a job they are actively recruiting for.

To Work or Not to Work with Recruiters?

Now that we understand the role of recruiters, we can deduce that it is inefficient to spend hours sending them hundreds of resumes. If we were to do that we would rely on the unrealistic hope that the recruiter is actively recruiting for a position for which we are a great candidate at this moment in time. We cannot build an effective job search on wishes. We should also not confuse recruiters with career counselors. We cannot expect a recruiter to look at our resume and give suggestions or to take the time to suggest which career path we should choose. This is not a recruiter's job and she will not be paid for that.

This does not mean that we should not connect with recruiters. It only means that we should do so more efficiently than in an email blast. If we would like to connect with recruiters, LinkedIn is the most efficient and least intrusive way. Most external recruiters, and many internal recruiters, are open to LinkedIn invitations. Recruiters like to be connected to many people on LinkedIn because it enables them to do a substantial amount of research without having to pay the extra fees LinkedIn collects for its fee-based services. Recruiters also often use LinkedIn Groups to find, connect with, and monitor good potential candidates, so join the professional and industry associations appropriate for your practice area.

What should I do if I find a job posted online by a recruiter and I believe that I am a great fit for it? Then it makes sense to send my resume, correct? Yes and no. Before clicking the send button, I would do some research and see who the recruiter is, whether he is exclusive or whether the job is advertised somewhere directly without the recruiter as a middle man. Any hiring partner would rather not pay a $40,000-$70,000 premium to hire an associate who is currently unemployed for a position that was nationally advertised right on the law firm's own website. This is especially true when that hiring partner has a stack of resumes piled up to the ceiling of similarly credentialed lawyers that applied directly to the position without a recruiter. If we can apply directly for the position, we should consider not going through a middle man, unless, of course, we have a well-established relationship with that recruiter. So, as always, finding proper information before acting is the key.

Short & Happy

- Recruiters are not working for you, the job seeker, but for the hiring firm. It is the firm that pays recruiter fees. It is the firm, their client, who they ultimately must satisfy. Recruiters do not earn money by helping you find employment.

Law School Resources

Another source of information is your law school's career center. We already invested a great deal of money at our law school, so why bypass the career resources they offer? Again, the role of career services staff is greatly misunderstood. They are a resource and not a place to unload responsibility. We cannot expect to have career services staff do the work for us. They are guides who help us navigate. Working with a career counselor can help us identify which resources need to be a part of our job search strategy.

The most familiar resource is on-campus interviewing. Almost all law school career centers bring employers on campus to interview students. While many law firms generally concentrate on those near the top of the class, some law schools distribute their on-campus interviews through a lottery-type system.

In addition, schools offer school-specific online job postings and alumni networking programs. Besides official programs, career services sometimes connect current students with alumni to facilitate networking and mentoring. Some schools even keep in continuous conversation with potential employers.

Schools also offer many counseling services, and everyone should take advantage of the career center's resume and cover letter services. It always pays to have a second pair of eyes review our product.

Another great resource is the career center's mock interviewing service.

At the end of the day, career services offices offer another opportunity of having conversations with professionals in the industry. Career services offices know the legal market and can provide invaluable information. So, go to your career services office tomorrow and start a conversation.

Short & Happy

- Law school career services offices are a resource and not a place to unload responsibility.

- Career services staff are guides who help you navigate the job hunt. You cannot expect to have career services staff do the work for you.

The Hidden Job Market

It is well known that we find ourselves in a time in which we are more likely to score a job through the hidden job market than through regular channels. The hidden job market is a term used to describe jobs that are not posted online or are otherwise advertised. The numbers vary but somewhere between 60% and 80% of jobs are derived through this hidden market.

Why would employers choose to avoid advertising their openings? The short answer is to save time and money. Many employers choose to hire through their professional network to avoid the lengthy, expensive, and frustrating process of evaluating online applications. Choosing other channels is not only cheaper, but also leads to more quality applicants and fewer applicants that are completely unqualified for the position. Professional acquaintances understand the needs of the job and have a vested interest in recommending good candidates. This is especially true if the recommendation comes from within the firm because the recommender will be working with whoever gets the job.

Furthermore, law firms take more and more pride in the idea of a certain type of attorney succeeding in this particular workplace. It is part of their brand. Getting new employees via referral strengthens the continuity of the brand.

Finding a Hidden Job

If some jobs are hidden, how can we possibly find them? First, we must know where they are hidden. There is no single platform to which we can turn, otherwise we would not call it hidden. But they are not hidden for everyone—only to those outside the community. They are hidden within networks and shared between people, not interfaces. So, how can we find them? By being part of the community.

Do not assume that having a law degree automatically makes us part of the community. Being a member of the community is an active process that requires acting for the benefit of the community. Being a lawyer does not by itself benefit the community. We will discuss this in more depth in the next section.

Short & Happy

- The hidden job market describes jobs that are not posted online or are otherwise advertised.

- They are not hidden for everyone but only to those outside the community.

- Being a member of the community is an active process that requires acting for the benefit of the community. Being a lawyer does not by itself benefit the community.

Relationships

Relationships are a fundamental part of a successful job search. It is outside the scope of this book to dig deep into this topic. I highly suggest reading "A Short & Happy Guide to Networking" not because I wrote it, but because building relationships will alter your job search into something you cannot even imagine.

How Relationships Assist Our Job Search

The world is made up of people. We live with them, interact with them, and work with them. They are part of everything we do. What makes us think that we can find a job without them?

There are essentially three ways to find a job: through "formal means," such as job boards on the Internet or ads in newspapers; through direct application on our own initiative; or through social contacts. Mark Granovetter concluded that "personal contacts are of paramount importance in connecting people with jobs. Better jobs are found through contacts, and the best jobs, the ones with the highest pay and prestige and affording the greatest satisfaction to those in them, are most apt to be filled in this way."[2]

But why? What is it that makes social contacts the "best" method of seeking employment?

As we have already discussed, before we can act, we need information that enables us to act. To apply for a job, we need to have information about its availability. Remember that the actual transmission of information about job opportunities is a more immediate condition of mobility than any characteristic of jobs themselves.[3] Information can reach us through different channels, such as through the Internet, so this fact alone is not the whole story. It is the type of information that changes the game. We do not need just any kind of information, we need valuable information, and the value of information we receive through "formal means" is very different from information that comes through contacts. One factor that increases the value of information is the nature of the information received. "A friend gives more than a simple job description" says Granovetter.[4] He can share information about the culture, the circumstances of the hire, the subjective preferences of the hiring personnel, and any additional information that enables more intelligent action and can place us in a better starting position. He can also give us that information before others receive it.

The flip side of the coin of what makes social contacts so valuable is the information the employer receives. As we know from drafting our resume, the employer is not interested in every piece of information we provide but only those facts that are important to her. Personal contacts enable employers to "simultaneously . . . gather information and screen out noise, and are, for many types of information, the most efficient device for so doing."[5] The number of applications received from suitable prospects is often unmanageable for the employer, which is why applicant tracking systems are increasingly used to cut through the initial noise. Social contacts are an economical way of obtaining decision-enabling information for both the employer and the job seeker.

But that's not all. If the information received by the employer is also coupled with a personal recommendation, it places the employer in a much more comfortable position. Recommendations of trusted colleagues are like certificates. Don't trust the theory, let me show you a real-life example. Below is an email I received from a partner at a New York law firm:

> Dear Desiree,
>
> We are looking to add partners with international expertise in the following areas: XXX.
>
> If you come across folks in your network in the coming year who you can recommend we would appreciate it.
>
> The headhunter route has not been fruitful; the informal personal connections have been much better.
>
> I hope to see you guys soon!
>
> Warmest regards, XXX

"The headhunter route has not been fruitful; the informal personal connections have been much better." Employers have long recognized the value of social contacts in the hiring process. The sooner the job seeker understands that, the better positioned she will be.

This is not at all a new development. In the past, job seekers found opportunities through recommendations only; there was no Internet, and even earlier no job sections in newspapers. Paper applications developed later when job seekers started to find ways of making their job applications more effective and companies developed new ways of making the process of screening candidates for jobs more efficient. And the story goes full circle. Today, we live in a time where the open and interconnected world we live in distributes talent globally and makes it more and more difficult to stand out on paper. Because of the Internet and social media, more and more people gain access to the same information. The greater the number of people that gain access to the same information, the less valuable it becomes, and the greater the number of candidates that apply for the same position, the more competition we face. Relationships, therefore, again become more important. The ever-growing importance of social networks for employment opportunities is an inescapable fact.

So, we need information, we need valuable information, and we need to find an efficient way to receive such information. The most economical way to receive and spread valuable information is through people. The more connected we are with others, the better positioned we are to receive information, and the better our job mobility.

"Network-Inequality"—A Job Seeker's Achilles Heel

Networking emerged as a management training tool because people were worried about "network inequality." Network inequality is an inequality not because of our gender or the color of our skin but of who we are not connected with. If not being integrated into a social network would not have any disadvantages, no one would have worried about inequality. The very fact that they did worry shows how important a social network is. Precisely because those who are not connected face meaningful disadvantages, precisely because networking makes such a big difference in someone's professional path, we must talk about networking.

"Superorganism"

A strong network is crucial for job mobility and this is because of the information transmitted through its channels. But there is more:

It is difficult for a job seeker with just a few loose connections to see the full benefit of networking. It is equally difficult to explain to a job seeker the whole benefit of networking. It is so difficult because something happens somewhere along the way, from a few contacts to an entire social network. Something new emerges. And it is what emerges that makes networking such a powerful tool. It is not just an assembly of contacts that grows bigger over time. From the interactions and interconnections of the parts, entire new attributes arise.[6] Just as "[a] cake has a taste not found in any one of its ingredients," in a social network "the whole comes to be greater than the sum of its parts."[7]

Christakis and Fowler describe this as a "superorganism."[8] Have you ever seen a flock of birds flying in unison across the sky? Have you ever wondered who the boss in this group is and how she is telling other birds when to make a sharp right? "[T]here is no central control of the movement of the group, but the group manifests a kind of collective intelligence that helps all within it,"[9] say Christakis and Fowler. And that is exactly what a social network does: it helps all within it and takes on a character that is greater than the sum of its parts—a "superorganism."

Short & Happy

- You need information, you need valuable information, and you need to find an efficient way to receive such information. The most economical way to receive and spread valuable information is through people.

- If you are not sufficiently connected within the legal community, your job search will suffer from network inequality.

Summary

Use job boards, recruiters, law school resources, and relationships as a source of information and not as delegates for what is essentially your responsibility. All these devices, when used wisely, will give you the necessary information to successfully navigate the market. There is no need to look anywhere else.

---

1 https://www.pbs.org/newshour/economy/ask-the-headhunter/ask-the-headhunter-is-linkedin

2 Granovetter at 22.

3 Id. at 6.

4 Id. at 13.

5 Id. at 97, 98 quoting Rees.

6 Christakis, Nicholas A., and Fowler, James H. Connected: The Surprising Power of Our Social Networks and How They Shape Our Lives: How Your Friends' Friends' Friends Affect Everything You Feel, Think, and Do. New York, NY: Back Bay, 2011. at 26.

7 Id.

8 Id. at 289.

9 Id. at 26.

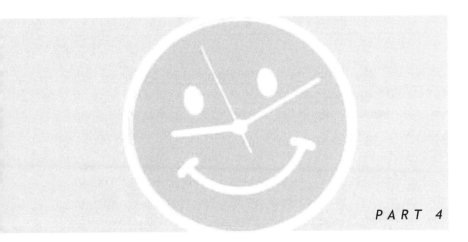

PART 4

How to Search

Online

The online world has become our reality. I am constantly staring into a device. So, we do the same when it comes to our job search. There is nothing wrong with it; to the contrary, the online world is a tremendous resource. Access to free information at the tip of our fingers is incredible. Can you imagine a time without the online world? I spent most of my teenage years offline and cannot fathom how I functioned without it. As job seekers we should absolutely use the online world but, and here is the important but, as *support* for the real world, not its substitute. The online world should be a tool to help us navigate the real world. It should not replace it. This is so important that I struggle with how to emphasize it. So, let me repeat it: the online world should be a tool to help us navigate the real world. It should not replace it.

Job Boards

How can the online world assist the real world? Let me use job boards as an example. The most common use of job boards is to look for open positions and to apply for them. This is, however, a very limited use. Why not use the information provided to come up with a more effective approach than simply sending our resume to an applicant tracking system? Let us have a look at what information job postings can give us. Granted, some postings are more elaborate than others, but some basics are usually given:

1. The firm that is searching; 2. Which position is vacant. This will also tell us about the department that is hiring; if it is a corporate position we can assume that the corporate department is searching. If we can deduce which department is looking for a new associate, we can, with a simple search, find the lawyers in that department; 3. We may find information about the person in charge of receiving resumes. And again, with a simple search we can find out what capacity that person holds, *e.g.*, is it human resources or a hiring partner? We can use all this information and move over to our next source: LinkedIn.

Enter the name and see whether one of our connections is connected with the aforementioned people. If so, and it happens to be a good acquaintance, why not ask for an introduction? If we do not have any close connections in common, we can check which associations they may belong to. Maybe we will find ourselves at the same event at a bar association in the near future.

These are creative ways of looking at a job posting. This example does not mean that this the only way to look at it. Be creative, take information, and put it to good use.

A job posting is much more than a black or white, apply or don't apply situation. It is one source of information, use it as such.

Keywords

Keywords are the words and phrases that we as Internet users type into the search box of a search engine to find those websites that match what we are looking for. While some keywords get hundreds of thousands of unique searches a day, others get a couple of hundred. High trafficked keywords are very competitive. You may be familiar with search engine optimization (SEO) and the painstaking search for proper keywords to include on a website. Keywords are very important for companies as they drive targeted web traffic to a particular business.

What does this have to do with our job search? If the person who wants to be found spends a lot of time and resources identifying proper keywords, should the searcher not do the same? Few job seekers spend time considering proper keyword search. To find proper keywords, there is a necessary preceding step—we must know what it is that we are looking for. If you are looking for a particular kind of shoe, you will not go to Google and type in shoe. This will lead to 1,300,000,000 results. If you want to find "Converse" you might put that term in. This will lead to 312,000,000 results. You refine again and search for "Chucks Converse," resulting in 19,400,00 results. If you were to search for Converse AND Chucks AND Grey AND 7.5 AND under $45, you would only get 456,00 results. You catch my drift? If you did not know that you wanted a Grey chuck in size 7.5 for under $45 you would have to struggle with 1,300,000,000 results.

We use keywords quite intuitively when we search the net. We even use full phrases or questions such as "How far is the moon?" (238,900 miles by the way). Yet, when it comes to our job search we use extremely broad terms such as "attorney jobs" (17,900,000 results). This just does not make any sense. This is the "anything approach," the "I want to be open to all opportunities" approach. This is where your job search turns into a nightmare. Let us stop chasing the elusive "anything" and decide on what it is we want to do, find the keywords, and search efficiently.

You also want to make sure that your search is organized. So, keep track of the keywords used in a spreadsheet. Some keywords produce better results than others and you want to keep a record of that.

Why Am I Not Simply Giving You a List of Keywords?

If I could I would. But the point is that keywords are based on one's search objective and without knowing it, I cannot give you a keyword. Search objectives are as diverse as people. A list of keywords supplied to you without having discussed important matters first is just as useful as the keyword "attorney jobs."

Boolean Strings

Recruiters are very familiar with Boolean strings—a search technique to get meaningful candidate results from a wide range of software. Boolean strings help filter search results to avoid an overload of data. A Boolean string may look complex but once the constituents are understood, they are easy to use. There are only five elements of syntax to understand. These are:

AND

For example, Associate AND Corporate will give results that include both the word associate and corporate.

OR

For example, Associate OR Counsel OR Attorney will give results that include one or more of the stated words.

NOT

For example, Associate NOT "Document Review" will give results that contain the word associate, but leave out any that use the phrase "document review."

( )

The use of parentheses causes the most confusion. Words within parentheses are given priority over other words around it. The most common way in which parentheses are applied by recruiters is in the use of OR strings. For example, we have a list of target companies we wish to work at, we can construct a command like this:

Facebook OR Apple OR Microsoft

But we do not wish to find just any job within these companies, so we might add:

"In-House Counsel" OR "Attorney"

We can now combine both commands into one search by using parentheses. This way we tell the search engine that we want to see results containing either "In-House Counsel" or "Attorney" and also one of Facebook, Apple, or Microsoft. It will look like this:

("In-House Counsel" OR Attorney) AND (Facebook OR Apple OR Microsoft)

It makes no difference which order the two sections in parentheses go; the same results will result either way.

" "

You will have noticed that I used quotation marks in the expression "Document Review" above. These quotation marks are used to capture a phrase that is to be kept intact, in the precise word order stated. Not using " " around a phrase will mean that each word is treated separately, usually with an assumed AND in between each one.

* * * *

By applying these elements along with our keywords, we can create a huge range of search operations. There is no limit to how often we can use any of these elements in a search, so we can create very specific search strings, which will save us a lot of time in filtering results.

Some job boards, such as Indeed, have advanced search features. Such features basically assist you in creating Boolean strings without you having to use any of the operators above. They offer the options to use "with all of these words," "with the exact phrase," "with at least one of these words," "with none of these words," etc.

Boolean strings are most frequently used by recruiters to search for talent. However, the sophisticated job seeker can make use of Boolean strings, as well.

Email Notification

Once you have used the proper keywords and a result-producing Boolean string you should subscribe to email notifications for these results. Many job boards offer this feature. This way you do not have to constantly check the sites. Relevant opportunities will be delivered to your inbox.

LinkedIn, Blogs, Twitter

I receive many questions regarding LinkedIn, blogs, and Twitter. Mostly, I am asked whether they are indeed as important as people make them out to be and what value the job seeker can expect to derive from them. LinkedIn (allow me to use LinkedIn as a synonym for all three sources to make reading easier) is extremely important but not for the reasons that many think. Many think it is a great way to be discovered. That is true, it is. But much more important is that it is a source of information. And a tremendous one at that—it gives information about people.

At my fingertips is all I need to know about my colleagues—where they work, what they do, what is important to them, what project they are currently involved in, what issues they care about, what concerns they have, what problems they try to solve, what makes them laugh, what makes them angry, and so much more. I can start a conversation with any person I meet about a topic that is dear to them by simply looking at their profile and online activity for a few seconds. Oh, how much that person will enjoy a conversation with me. Isn't it wonderful that I asked her about the Internet jurisdiction question in Europe that she has been so devoted to? LinkedIn gives me all that in a much more organized and accessible way than Google does. That is why LinkedIn is so important. It helps me navigate real life efficiently. Clients often tell me that they don't know what to talk to people about. Why don't you just talk about something the other is interested in? How can you find out about that? Look at their profile. This is so easy that it puzzles me that anyone would struggle with this concept. Talk about something that people care about which you can learn online. This is a situation in which people make the mistake of confusing easy with unimportance. Just because doing this is easy does not make it less important.

This is not to say that the chance of being discovered is neglectable. It is at the very least so important as to require us to have a spotless profile. Spend two concentrated hours on professionalizing your online profile. It is easy and important, so do it. Be sure that your social media accounts have suitable privacy settings and that you scrub any inappropriate content. More and more employers are searching the Internet to find available information on prospective candidates.

Short & Happy

- A job posting is much more than a black or white, apply or don't apply situation. It is one source of information; use it as such to come up with an effective search approach.

- Decide on what you are looking for and create a list of proper keywords to find results.

- Use Boolean strings to help filter search results and avoid an overload of data.

- Once your keywords and Boolean strings produce relevant results, subscribe to email notifications.

- Use LinkedIn, blogs, Twitter, etc., as sources of information about the players in the industry and not just a platform to broadcast your personal brand.

Offline

The Productivity Fallacy

Where should you spend more of your time during your job search? Online or offline?

The reason we are drawn to the online world and would rather sit at home hitting the apply button is because it makes us feel productive. We feel like we have accomplished something if we have sent out five applications. It is somewhat tangible. We opt for job boards and applications because it gives us a sense of control over the situation. Sitting in a committee meeting at a bar association seems like an utter waste of time when we should be applying for jobs, right? We do not have the time to meet for breakfast and lunch with other professionals because we need to find a job first, correct? Wrong! That is the "productivity fallacy." *Feeling* productive does not mean *being* productive. There is a huge difference. We feel productive because we make ourselves believe that this is what we should be doing to find a job. We have subscribed to the wrong idea.

Furthermore, what we should be doing instead seems so utterly ill-defined. Meeting and talking to people does not really lead to anything tangible. We cannot grasp the connection between a lunch and a job offer. Cause and effect are not properly connected in our mind. Applying → interviewing → job offer—this sequence is comprehensible and replicable. Lunch with acquaintance → chatting about a favorite theater show → interviewing → job offer is a sequence that does not make sense to us. The former makes us feel productive while the latter feels like a waste of time.

The problem is that application → interview → job offer is not a reality anymore. If it were, you would not be reading this book. This sequence may make sense in our head but is not updated to the current market. Competition has altered the game and we must adjust our approach accordingly. We must measure the opportunity costs between sitting in front of the computer and having lunch.

Opportunity Costs

Opportunity costs are defined as a benefit that must be given up to acquire or achieve something else.[1] Sitting in front of the computer gives us comfort because of the illusion of productivity—the feeling that we are doing something. When you are sitting in front of your computer you are giving up time in favor of another activity. Time is a resource and since every resource can be put to alternative uses, every action, choice, or decision has an associated opportunity cost. When it comes to online versus offline job search we must do a cost-benefit analysis. How will you spend your time?

Remember when I said, "faced with information that contradicts what we believe, some of us ignore the new knowledge and hold to their former beliefs, while others accept the validity of the new information and put it to use"? Whether you choose the comfort of the job board or schedule the lunch meeting depends on two things: whether you trust in what I say and how willing you are to give up your former belief. The choice is yours.

Short & Happy

- We opt for job boards and applications because it gives us a sense of control over the situation but *feeling* productive does not mean *being* productive.

- Time is a resource and since every resource can be put to alternative uses, every action, choice or, decision has an associated opportunity cost.

- Choose your activity based on what brings the best return on investment.

Building Relationships

We are social creatures. We have friends and our friends have friends, some who are also our friends and some who are not. We have family, each family member has friends, and these friends in turn have their respective families. We know our neighbors, we are members of a sports club, etc. We create all these relationships naturally and nurture them without thinking much about it.

Our circle of friends and family is a social network because our friends are points or nodes interconnected by communication paths. "Did you hear that Uncle Bob's friend Tim has a girlfriend who is 15-years younger than he?" This information passes through your family network faster than a speeding bullet. As social creatures, therefore, we live in and navigate networks every single day.

We not only live in networks and interact in our and with other networks every day, but we are born to do it. Our urge to connect and form into networks is hardwired into our genes. As Nicholas Christakis and James Fowler explain in "Connected":

> Among early hominids, individuals who lived in social networks that enabled a group to acquire more food or to fend off attackers were more likely to survive and reproduce. As a result, over a long period of time, the individuals who naturally formed networks or who had specific traits conducive to forming particular kinds of networks would have had a selective advantage and might eventually have made up the largest part of the population. The networks we form today exploit different tools . . . and operate in a different environment, but the urges we have to connect and to organize into groups of friends evolved at a time when genetic evolution favored some patterns over others.[2]

Because it is in our genes, we all are natural networkers. We do not need books or workshops explaining to us how to network. We need only to understand that building relationships is natural. All we are asking job seekers to do is to build relationships within the legal community, the community they seek to work in. You do not have to wait to work in the field to be a member of the community. You can be a member of a community by choosing to be one. A member of a community is not someone who solicits but someone who gives and shares. That's all. Pretty straightforward isn't it?

What Not to Do

One of the classic networking tips job seekers receive goes a little something like this: if you try to connect to a new contact, ask for advice on how to enter the field that the other is working in.

This tip is quite useless. Many emails are floating around the ether from job seekers who say, "I would love to hear your advice." How likely is it that someone can tell apart 20 job seekers all asking an identical question? Especially those in senior positions receive these emails on a regular basis. The message they have for job seekers does not change, only the person they are saying it to. How stimulating is it to be forced to repeat oneself over and over again?

After I speak at events, attendees usually come to me to ask questions. The most common of these questions is: "Desiree, I need to find a job soon, do you have any advice on how to approach the job market?" This happens 20 times per event, multiplied by many events per year. I have no way of telling these job seekers apart, even if I wanted to. If they approach me again at a later event, it's like meeting a new person.

Once, after an event and after repeating my "advice answer" for the umpteenth time, a person came to me and said, "My name is Rosa. You mentioned during your speech that you will be traveling to Madrid. I am from Madrid, here is my card. Let me know if you would like me to recommend some fantastic restaurants. Thanks for your talk." That was it. As we can see, her name is the one I remembered.

Advice Is Not Advice

Just to make myself very clear, I am not saying that asking for advice is a bad idea. Asking for advice is important and the ones that are asked will often feel good about being trusted for their expertise. However, there is a difference between asking for advice in a positive way and asking for advice in a negative or even destructive way, and these differences are manifested in several ways:

The first difference is timing: when do we ask for advice? Is it in the context of an established and trusted relationship or is the question asked to make an initial connection? Reaching out to a stranger with a "request" is contrary to how humans build relationships.

The second difference is the quality of the advice we receive. The typical question is "do you have any advice?" If we ask for anything, we will likely receive nothing. The value of the information we receive in response to an "any question" is very low. An unspecific question rarely produces a specific and useful answer. The answer will and can only be general. If we look at the question that I receive often "do you have any advice on how to approach the job market?" we can see that even under best intentions, I am not able to give a helpful answer. To the contrary, all I have is questions in return: in which field would you like to work, what is your expertise, how many years of experience do you have, what have you done so far, and so on. I could answer something like "you should develop a strong professional network and have a perfect resume." How helpful is this answer? It is neither helpful to the recipient, nor does it give me any incentive to begin a relationship with that person.

Furthermore, we should take into consideration what this type of question says about us as professionals. If we are seeking "any advice," we communicate that we either do not have enough information to be more concrete, or that we are not invested enough to be more concrete. Neither makes us look particularly interesting to the person to whom we are trying to connect. The more general our request for advice, the less impact our question has.

So, what should we do instead? Rather than asking for advice, we should ask informed questions—the emphasis being on "informed." By informing ourselves before we ask a question we not only show that we did what is required on our part before we burden others, but also that we are seriously interested in both the subject matter and the answer. If we fail to inform ourselves prior to asking, we burden others with what is essentially our responsibility. People are extremely happy to help and guide, but they are not interested in being burdened. In other words, people like being mentors, they don't like being secretaries to strangers. Asking for general advice is a mere fishing expedition; asking informed targeted questions is tapping into the value of a social network.

"Byproduct"

Job seekers make the mistake of building relationships with the intent to get a job. They misunderstand a crucial fact: valuable information, especially job information, is almost always transmitted as a byproduct of other social encounters, usually without anyone eliciting that information. The information provider is self-motivated. Let me repeat that: the information provider is self-motivated. To give you an example. I recently had dinner with four lawyers and their respective spouses. The reason for dinner was just a get together, to have some great Mexican food and margaritas. At one point one of the lawyers pulled out his phone, sighed and said: "I am so annoyed, we are expanding and need a handful of new lawyers and I receive these ridiculous applications. Can any of you recommend someone? I answered that I would send some names tomorrow. No one at the table solicited that information. The provider was self-motivated. This incident took two minutes. Two minutes out of many years of friendship and two hours of food and drinks.

If we start a relationship by asking for advice regarding our job search we may put the other on the defensive. We stifle the conversation and prevent it from evolving into an opportunity where crucial information is transmitted as a "byproduct" of a genuine relationship.

* * * *

Job seekers often try to force a benefit out of each contact and quickly lose faith in the whole process. It is this force, this pressure, that is counterproductive. Building relationships simply does not work under force or pressure. To the contrary, dealing and gaining trust with fellow humans requires ease and gentleness. If we trust and keep doing our work diligently and consistently, the collective intelligence in our network will emerge and help us eventually.

Building relationships does not require ingenious feats. We need only consistently apply basic social common sense. We do not have to force it, we do not have to be an extraordinarily gifted networker, we do not have to have a special social talent, we must simply apply basic principles consistently.

How to Get Attention and Interest People

One challenge many job seekers share is getting noticed. We often find it difficult to connect with strangers on a level that makes for a fruitful relationship.

When we discuss how to get attention, we obviously seek positive attention. How can we make ourselves heard and cared for in an age in which everyone is flooded with messages?

We can do so by being different from the majority. Being different is achieved by paying more attention to the person on the other side of the table. Too easy? Let me say it again: do not mistake "easy" for "unimportant." When I look at the emails I wrote in my first year of attempting to network, I cringe. I now understand why people did not respond. What was it that made these emails so bad? They failed to pay attention to the person on the other side of the table and did not provide an answer to the question "why should the other engage with me?" Today, I receive many emails from people I do not know, and they are almost always asking me to do something. One such example received over LinkedIn goes something like this:

Stranger: Desiree, it would be really wonderful if you could refer me to your network.

Desiree: Would you be so kind to let me know who you would like to be introduced to and why?

Stranger: I'd like you to refer me to those in your network who can point me in the direction of opportunities. I really need a job, my visa is about to expire, and then I have to leave the country.

This is obviously an extreme example, but even the ones that are better still do not induce in me any motivation to engage. Most of the messages I receive go something like this:

Dear Desiree,

I hope this finds you well. I came across your profile on LinkedIn and I am very interested in the work you do. I am a recent law school graduate from . . . I have interned at . . . and worked at . . . I am now looking for a job and it would be really wonderful if you could spare 10 minutes to share any advice you may have.

At first glance, the email looks decent, but let's think about this from the perspective of the recipient. I am hearing from someone I do not know; the message catches me at a moment when something entirely different than a stranger's job search is on my mind. My son may be sick, the deadline for a very important project is coming closer, and my dad's 60s birthday is this weekend and arrangements still have to be made. During this mess and out of the blue, this email pops up on my computer screen. The question is: why on earth should I go through the trouble of spending even 10 minutes to give any advice? I have 3 options: I can either write back and say I am sorry, but this is not a good time; I could ignore the message entirely; or I can try to help the writer of the message. Let's imagine that I agree to a phone call. How engaged am I really in helping the stranger? What is my motive for exerting any effort other than respectful kindness?

"You cannot ask anyone for anything without giving that person proper motive."[3] The emails above, like my beginner emails, failed to incorporate this advice and in turn produce dreadful results and unhappy networkers. When we look at how information flows through networks, we see that networking is something entirely different than simply sending bland and superficial requests in the hope of getting a 10-minute conversation consisting of advice that we might find faster on the Internet. If we want to receive truly valuable information, we first must build valuable communication channels and we can only do so through valuable relationships. There is not short cut to this. Let me repeat: if we want to receive truly valuable information, we first must build valuable communication channels and we can only do so through valuable relationships. The basis for starting a valuable relationship is *homophily*.

A Funny Word with Great Impact

Every relationship starts with interest. How do we gain one's attention and interest? Homophily. Homophily has powerful implications and if you live and breathe this principle, your networking will reach a whole new level.

What is homophily? Miller McPherson, Lynn Smith-Lovin, and James M. Cook say it like this: "Similarity breeds connection."[4] Homophily says that connections occur at a higher rate between and among similar rather than dissimilar people.[5] What is even more important is that "[h]omophily implies that distance in terms of social characteristics translates into network distance, the number of relationships through which a piece of information must travel to connect two individuals."[6] Consciously using this principle to our advantage will make for better connections and our networking more effective. That is why a struggling networker is always advised to spell out what things she has in common with the networking partner.

There are two types of homophily: status homophily and value homophily.[7] In status homophily, similarity is based on informal, formal, or ascribed status such as education or occupation. Value homophily is based on values, attitudes, and beliefs.[8] There are many dimensions of homophily that "are largely ascribed or strongly inherited from one's family of origin."[9] But there are also dimensions that "are to a large extent achieved."[10] The latter is where many familiar aspects of networking advice stems from, such as join a trade association. If we join an association, we create homophily with all the members of that association.

If we understand homophily as the desire to connect with those similar to us, we can begin with two suggestions:

1.   Start Close

We can make our first outreach more comfortable by beginning to connect to those that are "closest" to us. I suggest that job seekers prepare a list of contacts with all the people they already know. If we are networking beginners, we set ourselves up for failure if we directly start sending emails to the CEO of Google to see what happens. We can make our lives easier and networking more effective if we start with those that are "closest" to us, for example, people we graduated with, people on our sports team, in our wine club, in our office, etc.

2.   Trigger Interest

We can emphasize common ground and, thereby, trigger interest in the person we are reaching out to. It is not enough to merely state that we have the same interests; we must back it up with actions. If we merely state that we are interested in the other one's line of work but do not have any activity to back up that claim, we do not create common ground.

The easiest way to begin our networking is to start connecting to those that are closest to us in regard to status homophily, like education and occupation. "Almost a third of personal networks are highly homophilous on education.[11] So, when we reach out to someone who is a graduate from the school that we are currently attending or from which we graduated, it is important to mention that. Imagine a conversation with someone at a party and we tell her that we studied at XYZ and she responds, "What a coincidence, I did too!" You almost immediately feel some sort of connection to that person.

However, because education is a commonality shared with many, especially those in the same occupation, it is important to find additional commonalities. So, if you are member of the same association or worked at the same company it would be of critical importance to emphasize that as well.

But what if we are trying to connect to someone with whom we do not share any status homophily? When connecting to someone with whom we do not share the same status (in terms of homophily), we have to tap into value homophily: shared beliefs and values. Many experiments in social psychology have uncovered that attitude and belief similarity leads to interaction.[12] In my experience, connecting to a stranger is easiest when establishing common ground on things the other truly cares about. Many job seekers focus exclusively on shared education or work experience. Since we share these traits with many, they are less valuable in triggering interest. If we establish common ground with things the other truly cares about, we immediately create a strong bond. One word of caution though, since we are discussing professional networking, try to tap into shared professional beliefs and values and leave personal beliefs and values aside.

How "The Funny Word with Great Impact" Should Guide Our Networking

    1.   Due Diligence

Developing relationships is easy if we can find common ground with another person.

How can we find common ground with someone we do not yet know? Research what the other cares about—think of it as networking due diligence. If someone really cares about something, you can be sure that this is expressed somewhere on the Internet, on her website, a personal blog, Twitter, LinkedIn, or Facebook. If you follow someone's posts you can almost certainly identify what that person cares about, although inevitably some share more than others. Not many are willing to spend time on getting to know the other before they send out their first email. Those who research the other make an investment in the relationship that will set them apart from those who do not do so.

We can learn a great deal by studying how potential spies are recruited. Rarely does someone approach a foreign diplomat or similar person and ask: "Hey, do you want to be our spy?" An enormous amount of intelligence is gathered before the person is approached. Much of the intelligence is not gathered to find out whether the person would make a good spy, but to be able to approach that person with the best likelihood of her agreeing to join the team. Some might think, my goodness, what a reach comparing networking to recruiting spies. It is no reach at all. Former FBI agent Jack Schafer did exactly that. He used the knowledge he gathered as a behavioral analyst at the FBI and wrote the book "The Like Switch: An FBI Agent's Guide to Influencing, Attracting, and Winning People Over." Research before approach reduces the likelihood of rejection.

It goes without saying that we do not want to have a bullet point list of similarities in our email, nor is it enough to merely point to the same education. We need the sensitivity to know what to say and how to say it.

2.   Become Part

You will recognize another piece of advice that has its roots in homophily. Join bar associations! Space is the most basic source of homophily.[13] "We are more likely to have contact with those who are closer to us in geographic location than those who are distant."[14] The mere fact that you are in the same place at the same time for the same reason creates a bridge between you and the other. Joint committee memberships have powerful effects toward inducing friendships and the sharing of information.[15]

Many of the young professionals I work with are members of bar associations and frequently attend events. Their networking, however, is not going very well. Simply being a member is not enough to create a relationship. We must go a step further.

3.   Become Active

There are two different types of members in every bar association: those who pay their dues and are never seen, and those who pay their dues and devote their time, as well. It is the latter who reap the full benefits of membership in a bar association. "There is a distinction between co-location which puts people simply within range of one another, and co-presence, which implies a social relationship that is the framework of a . . . social structure," says Kadushin in "Understanding Social Networks."[16] When we attend events we are put in range with likeminded people but to fully realize the benefits of membership, we need to establish co-presence.

Co-presence is established by becoming active in the association. Bar associations offer countless opportunities to become active. The members of the committee I chair at the New York City Bar Association are required to submit one article each committee year and organize at least one program. "[F]ocused activity puts people into contact with one another to foster the formation of personal relationships."[17]

People say that 80% is showing up. It does not matter whether it is 50% or 75%, what matters is that it is not 100%. Showing up is a start, nothing more. We must become active.

If we keep the principle of homophily in mind, we will make our networking much more successful. However, even if we have a lot in common with someone, we still may not be able to form a relationship. This is normal and no reason to distrust this principle. We are not dealing with creatures of logic but with humans and relationships cannot be forced or manipulated, but rather must evolve naturally.

Short & Happy

- Homophily is the basis of great networking because of our natural tendency to choose people that are similar to us. Begin networking with those closest to you; it is the easiest way to find common ground.

- Homophily is the basis for important networking advice such as:

  - Do your research about the other;

  - Become part;

  - Become active and establish co-presence.

Resume Worthy Activities

Other than fostering relationships, which should take up most of our time, we should choose "resume worthy activities" for the rest of our available time. Just because we may be jobless does not mean that our resume cannot develop in the right direction. Drafting an article for the bar association's newsletter is resume worthy, staring at Indeed.com is not. Organizing a program about cultural challenges in international arbitration is resume worthy, cold calling a recruiter is not. We have the blessing and the curse of being able to choose how we spend our time. Choose resume worthy activities.

Short & Happy

- Do not wait for a job to develop your resume.

- Develop your resume while searching for a job by choosing resume worthy activities.

Branding Deeds

You probably have heard a lot about personal branding and its importance to career development. I agree that a personal brand is important, I disagree, however, that it is something that we can simply create by thinking about it. The way we interact with the world, the things we say and do, and the things we do not say or do, will create an impression of who we are and what we stand for. We can decide on all types of personal brands, but our actions or inactions will speak louder than words. It does not make sense for someone to ponder their personal brand while neglecting to send a thank you note for a resume review. You could say that I am holding a grudge, still complaining about that woman who never replied to my resume comments. But I am simply puzzled by the stupidity of this action—or better—inaction. If this person starts talking about her personal brand, I just want to pull my hair out.

Instead of wasting time trying to create a personal brand by thinking about it, we should watch our behavior and act in accordance with how we want to be perceived. Do we want to be a reliable, trustworthy, and competent professional? Well, then we must behave like one. Rather than focusing on being something outstanding we should learn to get the basics right.

Branding deeds are the actions that result in an impression of us. These can be good or bad. Everything we do or do not do brands us. We should create an awareness for the fact that our actions will lead to a judgment about our professional persona and we should act accordingly.

If you have a person that you admire then watch that person closely and mimic her behavior. You do not have to be a partner of a leading M&A practice to act like one. If she can write back within a few hours, so should you be able to.

Short & Happy

- Watch your behavior and act in accordance with how you want to be perceived.

- Branding deeds are the actions that result in an impression of us. Everything we do or do not do brands us.

- Your actions will lead to a judgment about your professional persona, so act accordingly.

Informational Interviews

We have already discussed the importance of information in our job search. The ability to seek information with a purpose and to be able to process that information cannot be exaggerated in its importance. After I have brought that point home, I am usually asked "So, how do I find that information?"

Our first instinct is the Internet. While this is certainly a good starting point, it is just that, a starting point. As I said above, the value of information decreases with its accessibility. Information on the Internet is accessible by thousands of people. How do we get the creme de la creme of information if not through the Internet? There is only one way, through people. And an informational interview is a conversation worth pursuing.

An informational interview is an interview conducted to collect information about a job, career field, practice area, or firm. As compared with a regular interview, the roles are reversed, and it is up to us to ask the questions.

Skillfully used, an informational interview is a valuable source of information. While it will cover some of the same information as on a firm's website, it presents opportunities for an inside view unmatched by other sources. Scoring an informational interview typically requires a lot of work on our end. We must convince strangers why they should take time out of their day to talk to us.

It is important to understand that an informational interview is not a job interview, nor is its purpose to get hired. We should not hope to receive an offer because of that conversation. The only purpose with which we should enter that conversation is to gather information through a mutually stimulating and interesting conversation. Even though informational interviews sometimes lead to employment, we should not pursue them with that expectation. If we were to do so, our attitude would prevent us from receiving the most important benefit—information. The interviewee will notice quickly whether we pursue the conversation out of a genuine interest in receiving answers to our questions or out of a hidden agenda to impress and score a position.

The informational interview is directed by our questions. The value of the conversation depends, therefore, on our direction entirely. Mastery of the art of skillful questioning is extremely important in this context.

Before

Before we reach out to anyone for an informational interview it is important that we identify the information we seek. And guess what, it requires that we know what we are looking for. We cannot use the informational interview so that the other can answer this question for us. The answer to this question is our responsibility. If you have made clear, in advance, the explicit purpose of your interview you will find your contact an interested and helpful person. Here are four steps to consider before the interview:

    1.   Make a List of People You Know

From that list choose a person that you are interested in learning from—not a person you are interested in being hired by. We must have interest in the person who we reach out to. If our outreach is not based on genuine interest, we should refrain from asking for her time.

    2.   Make the Appointment

We must perfect the art of the ask. A good email answers *why*, *what*, and *when*. We must demonstrate *why* we really want to meet with this person. Just because someone is in a higher position is not enough. Do we admire her career path? Do we think the work she is currently involved in stands out as the best? Maybe we have a shared connection and think she would be a great voice of wisdom. We absolutely must communicate specifically why we are reaching out to this person. The more personalized our ask feels, the greater chance of success we will have. Our email should also clarify *what* we are asking for. For 20 minutes of her time, for instance. *When?* We suggest a specific time but leave room to change at her convenience. Most people will be more than happy to talk to you but do not get discouraged if you find some people are just too busy to give you an appointment.

3.   Do Your Homework

Know as much as possible about the person, her area of practice, and her firm before the interview so you can ask informed questions.

4.   Plan an Agenda for the Session

This is your meeting. Do not assume the person will give you the information you need unless you ask the right questions. Select questions that will give you the most information.

During

An informational interview is a business appointment and we must conduct ourselves in a professional manner. We dress and act the role of a practicing attorney. Warm up with a little small talk first. If you do not know how to do that, you can easily practice it in your everyday life—in the subway, or with the mailman, or the taxi driver. After we have made some general conversation, it is time to move on to what we came for: the advice we cannot get anywhere else.

People love to talk about themselves, so when you first sit down, encourage the other person to talk by asking a question about their experience. It goes without saying that we should show genuine interest in her answers—her expertise and experience. This is an opportunity to listen and learn, not to pitch oneself. Let your understanding   of   the   informational   interview   and   your professionalism do the pitching for you. If we have knowledge of a certain field, and we want to show it, we can preface questions with what we already know. For example, "It looks like recent developments in the court's rulings are going to be pretty disruptive to the gas industry. How do you think this will affect your practice?" We must go with the flow of the conversation and not fire off as many of our prepared questions as we can. Rather than interrogating we want to converse in the most pleasant and natural way for both participants.

We should also be prepared to answer questions about what we are looking for. This is where we can really stand out. By being able to communicate precisely and efficiently what we are seeking and what our goals are in our career we demonstrate traits that are rarely displayed by job seekers. We do not ramble on about this and that. No maybes, no "I am not sure."

We should bring a resume, but do not offer it unless we are asked for it. Remember, this is not a job interview.

After the conversation, we ask for other names in the field she suggests we should have a similar conversation with. The key here is to make your request as specific as possible. We want to make it as easy as possible for our contact to think of someone. It is easier to think of someone when we ask, "Could you recommend a couple more people for me to speak with to learn more about reentering the workforce after maternity leave?" than to come up with an answer to, "Is there anyone else you would recommend that I speak with?"

Be efficient, do not overstay your welcome, be grateful, and express gratitude for the time spent with you. Depending on the billable hour, this conversation was extremely expensive for her. Always remember, the purpose of this interview is to obtain information.

After

The conversation may end at the door, but the relationship has just begun. Do not let this conversation be the end of it. We send a thank you note and we keep in touch about our progress. We share noteworthy progress and tell her when we implemented advice we received from her. This is not only a fantastic way to stay in touch, but it shows that we truly appreciate the advice and care about the other enough to share our success with her. And we absolutely must take advantage of any referrals that we received.

The following questions are intended to inspire you. Your own questions will arise naturally if you are genuinely interested in the other person. Your interview will be most effective if you formulate questions that reflect your genuine curiosity about her career.

Informational Interview Example Questions

- How did you get your start in this field?

- What is it like working at your firm?

- What projects are you working on right now?

- How do you describe the atmosphere/culture of your work place?

- What are the tasks performed during a typical day? Week? Month? Year? Do you have a set routine?

- What is your opinion on [exciting development in the law]?

- What is the most rewarding thing about working in this practice area? The most challenging?

- What are the demands and frustrations that typically accompany this practice area?

- How can you determine that you have the ability or potential to be successful in this practice area?

- What are the most satisfying aspects of this practice area?

- What are the greatest pressures, strains or anxieties in this practice area?

- What are the toughest problems and decisions with which you must cope?

- What are the dissatisfying aspects of this practice area?

- What are the main or most important personal characteristics for success in this practice area?

- My background is [. . .]—how do you think I can best leverage my previous experience for this practice area?

- What advice would you give me about how to best prepare for job interviews?

- What experiences, skills, or personality traits does your firm look for in new hires?

- What do you wish you had done differently when you first started at your firm?

- What job search advice would you give to someone in my situation?

- Which skills are most important to acquire?

- Where might job listings be found?

- What do you know now which would have been helpful to know when you were in my shoes?

Short & Happy

- An informational interview is a valuable source of information.

- Remember that an informational interview is not a job interview, nor is its purpose to get hired.

- Master the art of skillful questioning.

- The informational interview is only the beginning of the relationship.

---

1   https://www.investopedia.com/terms/o/opportunitycost.asp

2   Christakis and Fowler at 216.

3   Author Unknown

4   Mcpherson, Miller, Smith-Lovin, Lynn and Cook, James M. Birds of a Feather: Homophily in Social Networks. Annual Review of Sociology 27.1 (2001): 415-44 (415).

5   Id. at 416.

6   Id.

7   Id. at 419.

8   Id.

9   Id. at 426.

10 Id.

11 Id. citing Marsden.

12 Id. at 428.

13 Mcpherson, Smith-Lovin, Cook at 429.

14 Id.

15 Id. at 433 citing Caldeira and Patterson.

16 Kadushin, Charles. Understanding Social Networks: Theories, Concepts, and Findings. New York, NY: Oxford UP, 2012 at 18.

17 Mcpherson, Smith-Lovin, Cook, at 431 citing Feld.

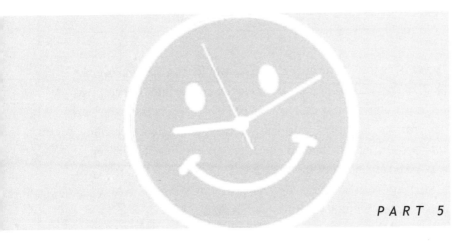

PART 5

How to Apply

Your Professional Persona

When we think about our job application, we immediately think about a few documents: cover letter, resume, transcripts, and writing sample. While these are part of a job application, they are just that, "one part." The most important part is neglected by almost every single job seeker: their professional persona. Everything we do, everything we say, and our mannerisms at all times form part of our job application.

What does this mean? It means that each of us is evaluated not only by the formal pieces of our application packet—particularly the resume and cover letter—but that we also will be judged by the other ways in which we act in any number of circumstances.

When we attend a function, for instance, do we arrive on time? Do we interact and engage appropriately with colleagues? Are we dressed in a manner suitable to the setting? Do we look after our manners and limit our alcohol intake? These are all among the factors that go into the impression that others have of us.

The same is true throughout the process of looking for employment (and, of course, beyond). Do we reveal emotional intelligence, have we cultivated strong habits of professional identity, do we demonstrate integrity, judgment, civility, enthusiasm, humility, commitment, humor, and authenticity? Are we reliable individuals who take responsibility for our careers? Do we have the ability to work well with a range of constituencies? Do we follow up appropriately with those with whom we have met?

With all the things that we will discuss further, never forget your professional identity. It is the biggest part of your job application.

Applicant Tracking System

Our application will likely reach an Applicant Tracking System (ATS) at some point. So, let us discuss this first. ATS are just beginning to become an essential part of the hiring process and it will be part in one way or another of every law firm hire in the future. There will never again be a time without an ATS. So, what is it and what does it mean for us, the job seeker?

ATS evolved from being merely a method of scanning paper resumes to store in a database, to a wide range of software options, some that focus on automating as much as possible while others assist the hiring partner to make her own decisions. In either case, the ATS is not meant to replace human decision making. Instead, its goal is to streamline the hiring process and make it more efficient so that the hiring team has sufficient time to focus on the human questions of the hire.

Features vary from one ATS to the next, but most allow for submission of job listings to multiple platforms with a single submission, to collect and organize job candidates in a LinkedIn style environment, and to break down resumes and present the data they contain in a standardized form which makes comparison easier.

They also automatically filter out nonsense applications. These, again, are not to replace but to make human judgment swifter.

What are we to take away from this development? It does not mean what the majority take it to mean—that we must alter our application and include keywords to bypass the ATS. This is nonsense. Either you have the skills for the job or you don't. The key takeaway is that before we hit the apply button we should honestly assess whether the job and our profile are a true match or just a desperate attempt to get lucky. We do not want to be one of those nonsense applications the system was designed to filter out. Hiring personnel get so many irrelevant applications that they need technology to cut through the noise. We do not want to be noise, we want to be the right tune.

Remember we talked about opportunities in Part Two? If we focus on real opportunities, our application will naturally "bypass" the ATS because we are a natural match. Whenever we feel like we are unnaturally squeezing keywords into our resume it should be a red flag that this may not be a genuine opportunity.

Know what an ATS is, know that it is there, and then forget about it and do your work.

Short & Happy

- An ATS does not replace human decision making. Instead, it streamlines the hiring process and makes it more efficient.

- The existence of an ATS tells you that you need to honestly assess whether the job and your profile are a true match or just a desperate attempt to get lucky.

Cover Letter

We will now talk about the actual documents used in applying for jobs. Please remember that the strength of our application is proportionate to the amount of information on which it is based. The less our application is based on information and rather on assumptions and guessing, the weaker it becomes. Yes, we learn on the job, but we should have a crystal-clear picture of what exactly the job demands before applying.

Do we really need to send a cover letter? The answer is yes! Even if an employer does not ask for a cover letter, we will send it. The cover letter is a professional letter and as such should comply with business letter formatting. How to do that is easily googled and does not deserve any more consideration here.

What does deserve some consideration, however, is substance. The cover letter, as the name suggests, covers the application and naturally comes first. However, hiring personnel may decide to read the resume first and then the cover letter. Some may decide to only read it if the resume is interesting, others only if they decide to interview us, and others do not bother to read it at all.

The cover letter is a one-page document that, along with our resume, is sent as our job application. A cover letter is our chance to tell a potential employer why we are the perfect person for the position and how our skills and expertise can add value to the firm.

Many do not understand in what way this is different from the resume. What can the cover letter possibly say that the resume is not already saying? Our skills are perfectly listed in reverse chronological order on our resume. Should we just repeat it in letter format thereby showing the employer that we can write full sentences? Absolutely not! The cover letter's purpose is different from the purpose of the resume and not simply a means to torture us but to give the employer information that is not apparent elsewhere. It tells the employer a lot about our way of thinking. To master the cover letter, let us tackle some facts at the outset:

> Fact number one: The employer does not want to read in the cover letter what she can already see on our resume.

> Fact number two: The employer is not interested in how well this job would fit into our career plans.

> Fact number three: The employer is a human just like us and as such primarily interested in her own concerns.

What does this mean for our cover letter? The employer wants to know how what we did in the past will help her in the future. In what precise way do our credentials fill the employer's current and future needs? The cover letter creates a bridge between our past and her future. The most common cover letter mistake is to only talk about oneself; what we did and what we want. Standard lines include: "I think the job would be wonderful for me because . . . ."

The resume, on the other hand, talks about our past from which the employer has to make the mental leap into the future. If she reads that we worked on multiple contract negotiations in the past, she will deduce the level of our future negotiation skills based on the number of years we practiced that skill.

In the cover letter we spell out this connection from past to future. We spell out how certain tasks that we have accomplished in the past translate into skills valuable for the employer's future. By spelling out how our credentials enable the employer's future, we likewise show that we understand the demands of the position for which we are applying. We cannot explain how our credentials will be helpful if we have no clue what everyday tasks the position demands. Many job seekers have no idea what the job they are applying for demands. As a result, they have no idea how to draft a cover letter. How can we tell an employer how we will be helpful if we do not know what she needs help with in the first place? It is not enough to generally outline responsibilities. Everyone knows that a litigator litigates. But what skills exactly are required for a successful litigator? What makes her and her firm successful? If we do not know the answer to these questions we better go back to our research. As discussed, informational interviews are the best way to get an insider's view into the everyday practice of law in a certain field.

Finally, our cover letter should demonstrate that we have done some research into what the firm's pain points are. An employer is not hiring because she likes to have more people around, she is hiring because there is a need that is not addressed. We are the solution to a practice group's problem and that is what the cover letter must show convincingly.

The heart of the cover letter tells the employer why we are the perfect fit for the job and we do so by spelling out how what we did in the past will be valuable in the future concretely. No platitudes, no guessing, no assumptions. Information is the foundation of a strong cover letter.

From this follows naturally a standard tip. A cover letter is customized for every single employer. Every employer is different and, therefore, requires a different emphasis of skills. If we send one cover letter to two different employers by simply changing the name, we do not understand what a cover letter is.

It is helpful to visualize the core of the cover letter in a table. In the left column write the employer's needs and in the right column you match it up with examples from your past. Once you see your skills and the employer's needs matched up, drafting the body becomes much easier.

The Basic Elements of a Cover Letter

Greeting: Address your cover letter to the proper person.

Opening: The opening functions as an introduction as well as a highlight. I suggest writing the opening last, even though it comes first. It is very difficult to highlight without having written the body yet. After we have spent considerable time with the core of the letter, the opening will be much easier.

Body: Relate your past achievements to the job you are applying for. How does your past benefit the employer's future? Be as specific as possible.

Close: Briefly recap your strengths as a candidate for this position, include your contact information, thank the reader for her time, and include a call for action.

Short & Happy

- The strength of our application is proportionate to the amount of information on which it is based.

- The employer does not want to read in the cover letter what she can already see on your resume.

- The employer is not interested in how well this job will fit into your career plans.

- The employer wants to know how what you did in the past will help her in the future. The cover letter creates a bridge between your past and her future.

Resume

You will hear so many different opinions about the style of the resume. Some prefer a certain font, others like a summary at the top while others hate it. We will not be able to please everyone's taste. And it doesn't matter anyway. What matters is that our resume fulfills its purpose.

The purpose of a resume is to outline our experience in such a way that it enables the reader to quickly and easily get a sense of our skill set and our professional persona. The emphasis is on quickly and easily. There are a few "rules" to keep in mind in achieving this goal.

10 Rules to Keep in Mind

1.　Be selective

The very first undisputed rule is that we should not put everything we have ever done on the resume. Our resume is not a comprehensive list of our career history, but a short pitch to demonstrate that we are the perfect person for the job. Therefore, for each resume that we draft, we highlight only the accomplishments and skills that are most relevant to the job at hand. We can keep a "master list" of our experience in a separate document from which we can draw elements into our resume.

2.　No need to state your objective

The second rule is not as steadfast as the first, but most prospective employers are not particularly interested in an objective statement. Save the space to focus on what really matters.

3.　Be conventional

The third rule is to keep it simple and conventional. So, keep the resume in reverse chronological order. There are lots of different ways to organize the information on your resume and you will find many different types of resume formats but in the legal profession, the reverse chronological order is your best bet.

4. Pay attention to the length

The fourth rule is a hotly debated topic—whether to keep the resume on one page. The bottom line is simple: the employer is looking for concise information that allows her to decide quickly. Being brief and concise is a skill. This is why Mark Twain said: "I did not have time to write a short letter, so I wrote a long one instead." If you truly have enough relevant and important experience, education, and credentials to showcase on more than one page, then go for it. But it is a judgment call that requires us to look beyond our self-centered world view. Naturally, we feel that everything we have done is important. But others look at our information with the same self-centered world view. The reader deems important only what is important to her. So, whenever we have to judge whether information should be on the resume, we must judge this from the perspective of the prospective employer. If we can tell the same story in less space, we must do that. If the employer reaches a second page, she will evaluate our judgment regarding that page with much scrutiny.

5. Use conservative formatting

Be conservative with the formatting. The purpose of formatting is to assist skim-ability, not to showcase our design skills. Be consistent but do not overuse italics or bold face. You should acquaint yourself with the basics of formatting, for example, the proper use of tabs rather than using spaces. This is especially embarrassing if we pride ourselves with Microsoft Word skills on our resume. And it is also for your benefit. It is a nightmare to edit a resume whose layout was achieved by hitting the space button a trillion times.

6. Make your contact information prominent

The sixth rule is to make your contact information prominent. We should include our phone number and a professional email address (not snoopy57@yahoo.com). We can include other places the employer can find us on the web, like our LinkedIn profile and Twitter handle, as long as they are 100% professional.

7. Omit summary of skills

The seventh rule is to omit the skill summary. If we have buried our skills under useless information, our resume is inadequate, and a skill summary will not save it. Skills should be apparent from the information provided on the resume. A summary is not necessary.

8. Be efficient and careful with word choice

The eighth rule is to choose words carefully. Every word in the resume should have a meaning and deserve the space it takes up on the page. Writing something like *provided assistance* is a waste of space since the same can be said with *assisted*. Take pride in being concise.

9. Be as specific as possible

The ninth rule is that every sentence in our resume should state something pertinent and should never raise a question. For example, "worked closely with senior attorney" raises questions without stating anything meaningful. What did you do exactly when you *worked closely* with the senior attorney? Did you clean her desk? Did you print her documents? Did you do legal research? Typical words that one can find in a resume that do not say anything are: attended, provided assistance, supported, worked closely with, prepared various documents, helped multinational organizations. How did you support, by bringing the coffee? Does "various documents" include shopping lists and holiday cards?

10. Show, don't tell

And finally, show rather than tell. Our experience section should show the reader what we bring to the table. There is no point in saying that we have "outstanding due diligence skills" when our resume is permeated with mistakes. We are lawyers, and we know that we must back up our claims with evidence. It is not enough to make bald assertions. The same is true with the resume. We cannot merely state that we are team players; we must show examples in which we exhibited that trait. Delete all buzzwords such as "effective communicator" or "strong leader" from your resume. They are meaningless. Show, don't tell.

The Experience Section

The experience section should always reflect the two R's: Recent and Relevant, and how they interact with each other. What is considered "recent" is debatable, but one thing is for sure: if there is a choice between including one more legal internship from 10 years ago or going into more detail about our current role, choose the latter, unless, of course, the previous job was particularly relevant to the one we are applying for. The experience section does not have to be balanced in that every job deserves the same amount of space. By allocating different space we place an emphasis on what is important for the particular position that we seek. A balanced resume can quickly become unfocused.

A common concern is what to do if we do not have any relevant experience. Then we look at our transferable skills. Transferable skills are those that were not acquired through direct work experience in the field in question but are nevertheless important skills that can be transferred. It is important to pair such a resume with a strong cover letter.

Rather than simply listing our job responsibilities we should think in terms of accomplishments. The legal profession is looking for performers. We want to show that we didn't just do stuff, but that we got stuff done! We should think about the benefits our actions had. We combine this part with figures and numbers. Look at a resume that includes numbers. You will notice that they jump out and draw attention. Be careful though that the numbers are indeed impressive enough to be in the resume. Applying at a top-notch NYC law firm and bragging about a $10,000 deal will hurt more than it helps. Quantify your accomplishments whenever you can and when they will add value.

Finally, do not neglect "non-traditional" work such as volunteering, writing, etc. Experience can be gained through multiple means, not just full or part-time employment. Remember to include your resume worthy activities.

Skills, Awards, and Interests

Foreign language skills absolutely should be on your resume. Microsoft Word or Excel skills should not. If you put Word on your resume you are actually saying that you have no clue about technology. Microsoft Word is standard. I had a long discussion with a law professor regarding Excel. He believed it belonged on a resume, I said it should not be on it. We agreed, finally, that you should add it if it is pertinent to the position for which you are applying and only if you have Excel skills that go beyond being able to create and use a standard table.

Feel free to show some personality and include an "Interests" section on your resume, but only add those that are actually interesting. Cooking, hiking, and traveling are a snooze. Are you a drummer in a local band, a sports pilot, or a weightlifter? I included in my very first resume that my interest was Poker. During an interview, I was asked whether I had a gambling problem. I was happy to be able to explain that I liked the mixture of psychology and the calculation of odds. We had a nice conversation about that and I got the job. Be careful with interests that are controversial.

Job Hopping and Gaps

Neither job hopping nor a gap looks particularly good on a resume. But our past is what it is, and we must deal with it on our resume.

Here are a few suggestions: if you can delete a short-term employment that was not temporary from the get go, do so. This does not mean you should lie about it. You must honestly address it in an interview should it come up. You can explain serial job hopping by including a reason for leaving next to each position, with a brief explanation like "company closed," "layoff due to downsizing," or "relocated to new city." By addressing the gaps, you will proactively illustrate the reason for your frequent job movement and make it less of an issue. If you have gaps of a few months in your work history, you can use only years (*e.g.*, 2010-2012) rather than months and years but you should do so consistently.

Four Tips to Format Your Resume Professionally

1.   Be consistent. Bolding, italics, and tabs should be used consistently to help the reader navigate the document, and to show your attention to detail.

2.   Save your resume as a PDF unless otherwise instructed. Some recruiters may ask for a word version of your resume. Follow the instructions to the letter. If nothing is instructed, send a PDF to ensure that your formatting remains intact.

3.   Name your file smartly. "Resume-Draft 6-Law Firm" is not a smart way to name your file. If this is for a law firm than there is another one for a company, right? That doesn't sit very well with a prospective employer. Save it simply with your name, *e.g.*, "Desiree Jaeger-Fine Resume."

4.   Proofread, proofread, proofread. Do not rely on spell check and grammar check alone—it can miss the worst mistakes. Ask family members and friends to look at your resume.

* * * *

Do you remember the discussion in law school about the living constitution? Well, the resume is definitely a living document. It grows with you and, therefore, requires constant care and updating. You do not want to spend a long night working on your resume because you promised it to someone in the morning.

Short & Happy

- The purpose of your resume is to outline your experience in such a way that it enables the employer to *quickly* and *easily* get a sense of your skill set and professional persona.

- Remember the two R's: Recent and Relevant

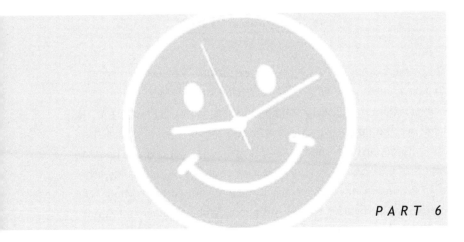

PART 6

Nailing the Interview

Before the Interview

The interview is not the end of our job search, but the beginning of a relationship. It is the first conversation that we have with our future colleagues. The goal, therefore, is to have a nice conversation—a conversation that our counterparts would like to continue.

The interview comes down to something very simple: the interviewer has already determined that our experience is worth a conversation. Now she wants to know whether we are colleagues others want to be surrounded with every day. Who does not want to work with nice people? Have you ever heard of "The Cleveland Airport Test?" The question employers ask themselves, among others, is "Do I want to get stuck with that person at the Cleveland Airport?" This is a good way to imagine the perspective of the interviewer(s).

There is no need to overthink the interview process. It is a conversation between professionals assessing whether they have rapport and whether they together can accomplish the firm's goals.

97

So, how do we prepare for this conversation? The very first thing is to know ourselves. Why are we sitting in this room having this conversation at this very moment? If we know why we are doing what we are doing, why we are having this interview at this firm, for this department and with this person, there is no need to rehearse answers. Obviously, the reason should be something other than "I need a paycheck and you invited me, so here I am." Our motive for having this conversation must go beyond our self-serving interests and encompass the interests of the other. It is a business meeting that assesses the potential for a business opportunity. We assess whether the proposal they make makes sense for us and they, in turn, assess whether our proposal makes sense to them. If we feel the need to rehearse answers it should be a red flag that the fit is not right. We should ask ourselves why an answer to a certain question does not come naturally. Most of the time, when we do not know the answer to an interview question, it is because we are having trouble explaining even to ourselves why we are a good fit for the job. If we have trouble convincing others, we are likely not convinced ourselves. Once we are convinced, it is easy to convince others.

The typical advice for interview preparation is to research the employer. As I said before, I find this advice a little troublesome at this stage. If we have not yet done this research, we have a problem. How could we possibly have drafted a proper application without having done our research first? Researching the firm or organization for which we are applying is extremely important, however, it should be done before we send our application, not after. The only thing we need to be doing at this stage is to refresh our recollection. We want to look into the person who is interviewing us to get to know her a little better. She should not be a total stranger when sitting in front of us. This obviously does not mean stalking her Facebook pictures but learning about her professional profile and speaking with others in our network who may know her.

Mock Interviews and Conversations

As a longer-term project, we should acquaint ourselves with the intricacies of the interview situation, especially how we react to certain questions, what makes us nervous or uncomfortable, what ticks we develop in stressful situations. Mock interviews are a perfect platform to learn more about our behavior under stress. If we have the opportunity to have mock interviews taped, I suggest doing this a couple of times. It is interesting to see ourselves on tape. You can always do this with your phone if you do not have access to more sophisticated equipment.

In addition to mock interviews, the best way to prepare ourselves for interviews is to learn to converse. After all, the interview is just a conversation. Granted, it is somewhat one-sided at the beginning with the employer asking the bulk of the questions, but the goal is a somewhat fluid conversation between us and the interviewer. If the interviewer leaves the room feeling that she had a wonderful conversation, we can rest assured that the interview went well. Have as many conversations with legal professionals as possible. The more comfortable we become in this environment, the easier interviews will be. Since informational interviews are a little bit more stressful than a regular conversation between professionals, they, too, are an excellent way to prepare for a job interview. That the roles are reversed does not matter at all. It is all about learning to be comfortable in a somewhat uncomfortable situation. Get yourself out there and converse. Know yourself and the employer, and you can sleep well the night before the interview.

Short & Happy

- The interview is a conversation between professionals assessing whether they have rapport and whether together they can accomplish the firm's goal.

- Remember "The Cleveland Airport Test." The employer wants to know: do I want to get stuck with that person at the Cleveland Airport?

- Ask yourself: why are you sitting in this room having this conversation at this very moment? If you know why you are having this interview at this firm, for this department and with this person, there is no need to rehearse answers.

- If you have trouble convincing others, you are likely not convinced yourself. Once you are convinced, it is easy to convince others.

During the Interview

Let us first discuss when the interview actually starts. The interview starts way before we sit down and are asked the first question. It starts when we approach the premises. From that moment on, we should be on our best professional behavior. Be courteous, nice, and friendly to everyone you meet anywhere in and around the building. This should go without saying but unfortunately it needs mentioning more than one might imagine.

We are not going to talk about dressing appropriately and being on time. For those who are professionals, this advice is just insulting. For those who at this stage need this advice, it is a lost cause anyway. It is common sense professionalism to be perfectly on time and to dress appropriately. As a career consultant, I do not work with anyone who does not have this minimal level of professionalism.

So, assuming we are on time and dressed well, what is it about the interview that makes it a topic we need to discuss? After all, it is just a conversation between professionals, as we have already said. But the circumstance in which this conversation takes place makes it worthy of discussion. As a job seeker, we feel pressure to make our case, to sell ourselves, and to show ourselves in the best possible light. Employment is a very important element of our lives and the pressure to secure a job, a good job, is intense. Moreover, we must deal with rejection. We will have interviews that will not turn into job offers and we must learn to proceed despite these rejections. These circumstances elevate a mere conversation between professionals to a stressful situation that can easily feel like an interrogation. The culprit is rarely the employer, but our own anxieties. As with many situations in life, it is more about managing ourselves, rather than others or situations. This fact should excite us very much since we are not left at the mercy of others. We can always work on improving our reaction to these stressful situations.

When things go awry, remember three things: relax, breathe, and smile.

Common Questions and How to Handle Them

1. Tell Me About Yourself

Often, the interview starts with four words we fear the most: tell me about yourself. This request to talk about ourselves without any frame of reference, without any guide posts, chokes many job seekers, even though we know it is coming. Should I start with my birth in 1981 or my great grandfather? Obviously not, but where do we start?

To tackle this, we need to mentally convert this request into a job-related request. What the employer really wants to know is "How did you end up sitting in this office at this moment in time?" Therefore, we start with the story that sets the stage for this particular interview.

For example, before I became a lawyer, I was an actress. I spent much of my teenage years in the entertainment industry. When I turned 25, I decided to leave the uncertainty of that business and study law. When I then was asked to talk about myself during my interview at a New York intellectual property law firm, I started with my acting career—not because it was an attention grabber but because the reason that I chose IP was to connect my new career as a lawyer with my past as an artist. In my past, I dealt with IP from the artist's point of view, now I wanted to deal with it as an attorney. Years after this interview, my employer and now mentor told me that this was the most important thing I said during the interview. I did not have any law related IP experience yet, I was junior, but I had a very good reason for why I was sitting in the office of an IP firm. It made sense.

So, why do employers not ask, "Why are you applying for this job?" That would be much easier. In medical study, future doctors are trained to ask their patients "What is going on?" The goal is to get a better overall picture of the patient without the patient fixating on a diagnosis she made herself, *e.g.*, "I have a cold because I have a sore throat." Her sore throat may be caused by something else entirely. The broad question "What is going on?" enables the doctor to make a more accurate diagnosis. The same is true for the interviewer: they want to get a better overall picture of us as a professional. No matter how young we are, we have a path that took us to this place and the employer would like to learn about it.

2. Do You Have Any Questions?

We have just covered the beginning of the interview. Let us now look at the end. Almost every employer will ask us "Do you have any questions for us?" We know this question is coming, so we prepare questions in advance. What could be the purpose of this? They know that we prepare for it, they know we know it. So?

The hiring partners I have spoken to had a very good answer. The interview is a conversation not a one-sided interrogation. For the bulk of the interview we are asked questions, so it is only fair to allow us the opportunity to ask questions in return. It is a matter of respect to not treat us as a passive and merely reactive participant. It reflects the double-sided nature of the interview.

We as job seekers are evaluating this job opportunity just as much as the employer is evaluating us. After all, we will be working at this place with these people for many hours to come. Don't we want to make sure that we would enjoy that?

When we are given the floor to ask questions, we should remember that the interview is not over yet. An employer once told me that he has seen many candidates talk themselves out of the job at the end. Good candidates know this is another time to shine.

It is imperative that we ask questions that do three things: first, show that we have done research about the firm. Second, mention something else relevant and interesting about us. And third, prompt an interesting answer and a good discussion.

We have covered the beginning and end of the interview, let us now look at the middle and a few common questions:

3. Where Do You See Yourself in Five Years?

We know that life turns out different than we may think, and many do not even bother making plans for tomorrow, let alone five years from now. Employers are not interested in our clairvoyance, but in whether we have a vision, whether we are determined and a proactive person rather than someone that simply reacts to circumstances. Do we simply wing it, or do we give our next steps some thought and align them under a common goal?

But since employers are mainly interested in themselves they want to know how they fit into our five-year plan. We, therefore, focus on the employer and include her in the picture that we paint of our future. In five years, we should have made a significant impact to the firm's practice and bottom line. We should think about how we can achieve this in the role we are interviewing for.

4. Why Should We Hire You?

Because the firm would be crazy not to. The employer does not want to hear how great we think we are. She wants to know specifically how we will serve the firm's goal. We also do not want only to meet expectations, we want to exceed them. So, we should include additional abilities. We may have skills that we noticed are in other job descriptions for similar positions. We may also have been down a path that they are currently embarking on. Having "lessons learned" and other strengths to offer a firm is a very strong plus for a job candidate.

5. Why Do You Want to Work Here?

The answer to this question has two aspects: the content and the delivery. Employers do not only want to know whether they *think* that we can fit in but also whether they *feel* that we can fit in.

Fitting in means that we possess not only the skill set required in the job description, but also a cultural fit with the firm. To be able to answer this question properly, we must know what the culture is. We need to understand the reasons why others enjoy working there and the best way to find this out is the informational interview, aka information gathering.

The delivery of our message must be genuine. If the employee feels we are just "telling them want they want to hear," the interview can be over in their minds. They want to know this is not just a job and a paycheck for us. They want to feel that this is what we want to do and the best place to do it. They want to feel some passion.

6. What Do You Know About Us?

Not knowing about the firm for which we seek to work is an indication that we are not very serious about working there. But it is also very much in our self-interest to answer that question. We will have to go into that office every day, likely for very long hours. Do we not want to know what this place is like? I suggest paraphrasing this question and answer for yourself "Why do I want to work there?"

To be able to answer that, we must know more than is listed on the firm's website. Simply reading through the website is not enough. The website is marketing for clients, not information for future employees. We must do some serious research. Read articles written by attorneys at the firm, articles written about the firm, blogs, and LinkedIn profiles. Maybe the firm has a LinkedIn group on which it discusses legal issues. Whatever it is, search beyond the firm's website.

7. How Do People Describe You?

Here is another opportunity to differentiate ourselves. Everyone claims to be a hard worker, a good communicator, and a team player. But how many are game-changers or leaders in the industry? No matter what it is, we must always have stories to back up our claim. The interviewer will want to know why someone thinks we are these things.

And again, we focus on them: we want to present attributes that make us sound like the go-to guy or gal wherever we work. Be aware, though, that we cannot simply state what is expected of us as a 21st century lawyer. Being an ethical and hardworking attorney is a given in this day and age.

If you need to use standard answers such as "People say that I am a good communicator," then at the very least go a step further. For example, being a good communicator does not mean just speaking well, it includes being a good listener. Maybe you hear things that others do not. Maybe you understand things quickly. Maybe you can figure out what people are trying to tell us through other clues, such as body language. This addition will make a standard answer more valuable because it reflects a level of emotional intelligence.

8.   What Is Your Greatest Strength/Greatest Weakness?

Our greatest strength should be something the employer needs. We do not choose something irrelevant to the job or the employer but focus on them: you may have many strengths, but we pick the one they need help with the most.

I dislike the "greatest weakness" question. Everyone knows that it is a trap, and everyone knows that the candidate is going to say something like "I'm a perfectionist." I suggest giving a genuine answer. Having weaknesses is not an issue, ignoring them and not working on them is. When you give a real answer, you are being genuine. You are admitting you have some growth opportunities and are not perfect. But I strongly suggest pairing the statement of your weakness with a plan to overcome this weakness through some training or practice. It shows the employer that you are able to self-assess, self-regulate, and self-manage.

9.   When Can You Start?

This question is encouraging but it does not mean that we have the job. We must keep our guard up until we clear the interview zone by a few yards.

If we are currently employed, we should be honest about the start date and show professionalism. We should tell them that we would have to discuss a transition with our current firm.

If we can start right away we can certainly say that we are able to start tomorrow. Excitement about starting work is always a good thing.

10. How Did You Find This Job?

There are two options in answering the question how we found this job: either we found the job, or the job found us. Either way, this is another opportunity to show the employer that we applied for the position for a good reason and not just because it was an opportunity for a paycheck. We can go into a little detail on what kind of job search we conducted and how the results informed our decision. We may have found the opportunity while researching jobs where we can make the most impact and hope to grow professionally. We should also have looked for firms that we feel meet our standards for culture, investment in employees, successful business model, and perhaps giving back to community. Include any other aspects you feel are important to you, but you absolutely must make sure that these are actually things the firm subscribes to. If we are listing a quality that the law firm never considered relevant, our answer will diminish our prospects.

The "job" may have found us. In that case, we can say that we were contacted by HR, a recruiter, or a connection in our network who felt we were a good fit. But we do not leave it with that. We should still mention that we did our homework and verified that this opportunity is indeed right for us.

11. Why Do You Want This Job?

It is obvious—because we need a job—but this cannot be our answer. The employer wants to learn more about the seriousness with which we considered this opportunity beyond the promise of a paycheck. Employers want to see devotion to the everyday tasks and the bigger goals of the firm that go beyond "everyone needs a job."

One thing to keep in mind with this answer and with every other is that even though the employer asks about our feelings, what she is really interested in is her firm. In the end, every question's purpose is tied to whether we sincerely want this job at this firm and do so for plausible reasons. It follows, therefore, that the reason cannot be about money, location, work schedule, or benefits because none of those are important to the hiring manager. Employers just like anyone else want to feel like their work means something to you and is not just the sum of various benefits.

12. Explain Gaps in Employment

A gap in employment is not a big problem if the gap was used well. We should make sure to paint a picture that we were productive and improving ourselves. Being unemployed and being latent are two different things. Employers do not like to hear that you had to recharge your batteries.

* * * *

Following are some questions that can get us into troubled waters. They key here is to keep the answers short. Many of us start to ramble when we get uncomfortable. Do not feel the need to expand your answer by including a lot of details.

13. Why Do You Want to Leave Your Current Job?

We should never be negative about our current position. If we say we hate our current boss or company, the interviewer will detect negativity and a lack of discretion. If we say that our current compensation or role is below our standards, they will question our values and genuine interest in the job.

Although these may be legitimate reasons to leave a job, we must talk about other reasons. Our current company or department may have become unstable or our current employer may not be able to offer us any professional growth. Whatever it is, we should highlight a reason the new employer cannot be concerned about. Furthermore, we should be positive about the new opportunity, rather than negative about the current position.

14. Why Did You Quit Your Last Job?

Typically, we should not quit a job until we have accepted another job. However, life does not always allow that to happen. Maybe we quit so we would have more time to look for our next job? Perhaps the firm we worked for was close to shutting down and we did not want to waste valuable time waiting for the last day of operation. There are common reasons that are understood as necessity, for example, a move to a new location, or family or health reasons. But we should be careful and thoughtful about the answer.

15. Why Were You Fired?

Being laid off does not mean that we were fired. Layoffs are typically not personal but business decisions. Most employers will know this.

Either way, we never defend ourselves or portray ourselves as victims. If we made a mistake, we must try to minimize the severity of the situation without bending the truth. An argument with a boss could be described as a difference in opinion. We never ever cast blame on others.

I highly recommend adding a "silver lining." Did we learn a lot from the experience and now possess knowledge that will mitigate the chances of this happening again?

* * * *

We cannot possibly go through every question an employer might ask and it is not necessary. Two themes should be apparent from the questions we discussed here. First, the employer is primarily interested in her professional needs and the success of the firm; and second, she wants to know how we can contribute to that success and whether we fit into the community. Every answer should, therefore, address these themes in one way or another.

Short & Happy

- A successful interview depends more on managing yourself than convincing others.

- Remember it is a business conversation not an interrogation.

- The interview can be the beginning of a new professional relationship; enjoy it.

After the Interview

Before we can address what happens after the interview, we must define when the interview actually ends. The interview does not end when we get up from the table. It does not even end when the interviewer says goodbye. It does not end when we step into the elevator or when we leave the building. The interview ends only after we have some physical distance between us and the employer's premises. We should never let our guard down. Being respectful goes without saying but sometimes nervousness or stress brings out the worst in us. We should stay focused and be ready to respond in a professional manner every minute.

Once we are home, we can relax a little and start preparing our follow-up. There is no question as to whether to follow up. We absolutely should follow up. The only question is how we should do so. There is some debate about whether to follow up with a written note or with an email. While some say a written note helps you set yourself apart, others say that a written note is just too cumbersome, and they prefer a brief email. The only advice I can give you is that not following up is a mistake and that you cannot go wrong by sending a professional email. Whether you can set yourself apart with a written note depends on who you send it to. Rather than losing sleep over whether to send a written follow up or not, let us focus on what really matters.

The follow-up should be brief, concrete, and professional. A follow-up does not have to be long, indeed it should not be long. A follow-up email that is copied and pasted from one email to the next is not only unimpressive but can be damaging. Employers have told me that they notice if their colleagues are getting the exact same email. Therefore, it should specifically address the particular person. Reference something you talked about during the interview. Make it personal not by talking about personal matters but by addressing each interviewer individually. Make a mental note during the interview of things said so that you can circle back on it during the follow-up.

Short & Happy

- The interview ends only after the premises have been left behind.

- Follow up with a brief, concrete, and professional note.

Hired

Negotiating an Offer

Job negotiations can be very complex and uncomfortable. The outcome can depend on who has greater leverage. Those who are unemployed feel they have no bargaining power. A weak labor market has left job seekers also with less leverage and has positioned the employer to dictate the terms. Nevertheless, there still is an opportunity to skillfully negotiate the terms and conditions of our employment. Deepak Malhotra, Professor of Business Administration at the Harvard Business School, has identified the following rules for a successful negotiation:

When to Negotiate

The first consideration is timing. When should we mention our salary requirements? We should not attempt to ask for anything before we have received an offer. It may result in our elimination as a candidate. We cannot start negotiating a non-existing offer. An offer is either a verbal or written statement that sounds something like "We would like to offer you the position of. . . ." Once we have received an offer, we show our enthusiasm for the job and ask how long we have to evaluate the offer. Once we have an offer, we hold some leverage. The firm wants us, and they have invested time in searching the candidate pool and selecting us.

What to Negotiate

We usually think about salary, but this is not the only negotiable on the table. Based on our needs, any of the following additional items may be negotiable: job title, start date, vacation time, reporting relationships, decision-making, level of authority, relocation expenses, memberships, bar association dues, subscriptions, signing bonus, performance bonuses, home office technology, flex-time, CLE costs, remote or virtual work, or severance provisions. Before we start negotiating anything, we should look at this list and select the items that are most important to us.

How to Negotiate

Research, Research, Research

We begin researching salary ranges before we start negotiating. We can use websites such as PayScale or Glassdoor, but the most helpful information usually comes from current or former employees. Ask people in your network if they were able to negotiate and what types of things they have seen colleagues negotiate at this or similar firms.

The Other Side of the Table

As we have said before, we should understand the person across the table. Before we can influence the person sitting opposite us, we must understand her interests and individual concerns. Negotiating with a hiring partner is very different from negotiating with an HR representative.

Understanding the Firm's Constraints

Before we start to negotiate, we should understand the firm's constraints. Some firms may have certain ironclad constraints, such as salary caps, that no amount of negotiation can loosen. Our job is to figure out where there is flexibility and where there is not.

Keep Perspective

We can win the negotiation but lose the job. Ultimately, our satisfaction hinges less on getting the negotiation right and more on getting the right job. Do not get caught up in the negotiation and insist on winning it. Do not let negotiations sour the relationship or, worse, result in a retraction of the offer.

Likeable

People are going to fight for us only if they like us. Anything we do in a negotiation that makes us less likable reduces the chances that the other side will work to get us a better offer. There will always be some tension in negotiations and the one who can navigate these fragile waters with the most grace has nothing to fear. We must strike a balance between asking for what we deserve and being greedy, between pointing out deficiencies in the offer and being petty, between being persistent and being a nuisance.

Proper Motive

We should never ask for anything without providing a reason. We should help the employer understand why we deserve what we are requesting. Liking us is important but not enough. We should not expect her to come up with the reasons by herself. We must explain precisely why our request is justified. If we cannot justify a demand, we should not make it.

Multiple Issues at Once

Regarding the negotiables mentioned above, we should negotiate multiple issues simultaneously rather than serially. It can be incredibly annoying to start with the salary and once this is resolved, adding "one more thing." If we ask for only one thing initially, we give the impression that we are ready to decide once that issue is resolved. Furthermore, if we have more than one request, by raising them together we can also signal the relative importance of each. Otherwise, the employer may pick the two things we value least, because they are easy to give to us. Now she may feel she has met us halfway, but we are not satisfied.

Never Assume the Worst

We should not fixate on words but always try to understand the other's motives and intent during the negotiation. Others are rarely interested in boxing us into a corner. They most likely have legitimate concerns they feel the need to have addressed. When confronted with these questions, we must focus on the questioner's intent rather than the question itself. For example, an employer who asks whether we would immediately accept an offer tomorrow may simply be interested in knowing if we are genuinely excited about the job, not trying to pin us down. A question about whether we have other offers may be designed not to expose our weak alternatives but simply to learn what type of job search we are conducting and whether this firm has a chance of retaining us. Even if we do not like the question, we never assume the worst. Rather, we answer in a way that addresses the motives and concerns behind the question. If we do not know what that is, we ask for a clarification of the problem that the interviewer is trying to solve. If we engage in a genuine conversation about what she is after and show a willingness to help her resolve whatever issue she has, both of us will be better off.

Do Not Play the Tough Guy

People do not like being told "or else." This is not the place to give an ultimatum. Instead of making demands we should ask questions. For example, if we ask for a higher salary we can form a question such as: based on my specific skills, I was expecting a higher starting salary. What can we do to increase this number?

But what should we do when we are at the receiving end of an ultimatum such as "We will never do this?" Then we should not dwell on it or make her repeat it. Instead, we should show understanding and say something like "I can see how that might be difficult, given where we are today. Perhaps we can talk about X, Y, and Z instead." If the ultimatum is set in stone, we should remember that what is not negotiable today may be negotiable tomorrow. Over time, interests and constraints change. When someone says no, what she really saying is "Not today." For example, if a potential partner denies our request to work from home on Fridays, she may have no flexibility on this issue, but it may also be that we have not yet built up the trust required to make her feel comfortable with that arrangement. Six months in, we will probably be in a better position to persuade her that we will work conscientiously away from the office. We should always be willing to continue the conversation.

Control the Pie Hole

There is an old saying: she who talks first loses. That is not going to be us. We keep quiet and always wait for an answer. When we propose our salary number or another item to negotiate we do not talk but wait for the response. Silence is very uncomfortable for many, so we tend to avoid it by filling the void with useless chatter. We must control that urge and give the other time to think and talk. Take comfort in silence.

Be Patient

Delays in the confirmation of a formal offer can be frustrating. But if we are far enough along in the process, the firm likes us and wants to continue liking us. Unwillingness to move on an issue may simply reflect constraints that we do not know about. Be patient but stay in touch. And if we cannot be patient, we do not call up in frustration or anger but ask for a clarification on timing, reiterate our interest, and ask whether there is anything we can do to assist in this process.

Win-Win Solution

Our goal is that both of us leave the conversation feeling good. Remember, this is the start of a relationship. The deal we cut should, therefore, be a win-win.

Be Prepared

. . . to walk away. If the offer does not meet our expectations in areas that are important to us, we may be better off declining the offer.

This Is Not the Time and Place to Be Sensitive

We leave our emotions at the door. This is a business transaction. We do not let our pride, fear, uncertainty, or any other emotion impact what we say or do.

Short & Happy

- Think about all the negotiables that are important to you and always keep the bigger picture in mind.

- Be prepared, be patient, don't play the tough guy, and do not let your emotions get the better of you.

Using One Offer to Secure Another Offer

It is tempting to use one offer to secure another, but we should always communicate that the employer can retain us if in fact that is realistic. No one wants to spend time and political capital to get approval for an offer if they suspect that we are still going to say "No, thanks." So, if we intend to mention other offers, we should make it clear that we are serious about working for this employer. We should balance the other offer by saying why we would be happy to forgo that option and accept an offer with this firm. The law firm with which we are negotiating should always feel like our first choice.

Choosing from Among Multiple Offers

At the beginning of a job hunt, we often want to get at least one offer to feel secure. This is especially true for people just finishing a degree program, when everyone is interviewing, and some are celebrating early victories. Ironically, getting an early offer can be problematic: once a firm has made an offer, it will expect an answer reasonably soon. If we want to consider multiple jobs, it is useful to have all our offers arrive close together in time. So, do not be afraid to slow down the process with one potential employer or to speed it up with another to have all your options laid out at one time. This should be within reason, of course. Do not pull back too much or push too hard. A firm may lose interest and hire someone else.

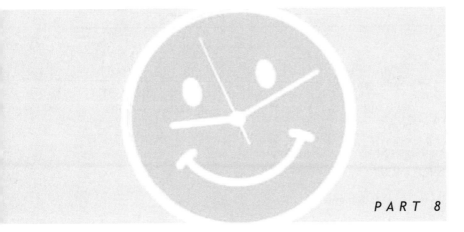

PART 8

The End of the Beginning

At the end of this book you will not have reached your job journey's end; you will not even reach the beginning of its end. But you will have ended its beginning.

Now, it is your turn to bring your job search to the next level. Remember that it is the little things that will make a big difference because difficulty is not always proportionate to importance. Be open minded towards every suggestion that comes your way. Be comfortable accepting ideas that conflict with what you have believed so far. And whenever things start to look dire and you start to feel again that you have no control over your job search, focus on these three things:

1. The importance of your objective. Identify and focus on your objective. Omit the word "any."

2. The importance of information. Information is the bedrock of your job search. Learn to find the clues, to connect the dots, to interpret data in light of your purpose. Seek the information that only a few have.

3. The importance of people. The world is made of people. We live with them, we interact with them, we work with them. You cannot do a job search without them.

I am excited about your job search because I know that it is in your hands entirely to make it work. Is this not exciting?

It has to start somewhere.

It has to start sometime.

What better place than here?

What better place than now?

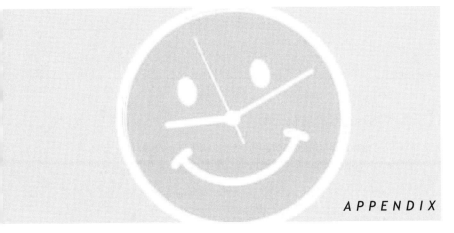

Short & Happy

Part One: Let's Get Started

Survival of the Fittest

- The person who will win is not always the person with the most assets but the person who uses her assets most skillfully.

- Working efficiently means knowing how to do things the right way but working effectively means doing the right things.

- Do not confuse familiarity with knowledge. Always be ready to learn something new in what you have heard before.

- Difficulty is not always proportionate to importance. In job hunting, it is the simple things that will make the difference.

- Be obsessed with the process and focus on its perfection. The goal can be reached only by perfecting incremental steps.

Failure

- Failure is an inevitable part of your job search. Learn to deal with it.

- Do not ignore failure but deal with it by extracting information that helps you improve in your pursuit.

The Loser's Game

- The job search is a Loser's Game.

- Job seekers do not beat the market by scoring points, but you may beat yourself by making mistakes and conceding points.

- Focus on consistent, mistake-free performance.

The State of Confusion

- Confusion reflects a lack of information.

- Find information that clarifies the situation and do not rest until you find it.

- Watch your attitude toward new information. If information contradicts how you perceive the situation, be open and accept the validity of the new information and adjust your behavior accordingly.

Response-Ability

- Responsibility can be abdicated but it cannot be delegated.

- Be comfortable considering your potential role in a problem. If you distance yourself from your potential role in a problem, you also distance yourself from your place in the solution.

- You have the ability to choose your response in every situation.

Responsibility is positive and empowering and not to be confused with blame.

Laser Focus

- Indecision is disabling. Decide!!

- It does not matter whether your decision is the right one in the end. What matters is that you decide.

- Being open to anything does not lead to more opportunities, it only blinds us to see what is right in front of us.

- Decide on a blue Mercedes today and you will see them everywhere.

The "Job Search in a Bubble" Syndrome

- Information is power. The transmission of information about job opportunities is more important than any characteristic of jobs themselves.

- Be an investigator—a collector and processor of information.

- Information is in the market and the people working in it can share more than any other information outlet.

- Do not dismiss information that contradicts your belief about a situation—embrace it and adapt.

- The more people who have access to the same information, the less valuable it becomes.

- Move from data to information to knowledge.

The Active Versus Passive Job Seeker

- Reactive people wait for things to happen to them, but they never make things happen.

- Move away from the job board centered job search approach.

- An energetic and active job seeker beats a passive job seeker every time.

- Be excited about the opportunity to create your future.

The "But" Person

- If you do not have the time to make your job search your priority, do not expect others to make it their emergency.

- Excuses communicate only one thing: incompetence.

- With every seemingly benign excuse, you make yourself less marketable. Stop making excuses!

- Do not seek other people's compassion, seek their respect.

- The frequency of the use of "but" is proportionate to one's failure in achieving success.

- Don't be a "but" person—a person who seeks others to validate their preconceptions.

Part Two: What to Search for

Two Roads to Nowhere: Anything and Nothing

- When you search for a job you must start somewhere and starting with anything will lead you nowhere.

- The search for "anything" is an outcome of indecisiveness.

- Your search object must be differentiated from your willingness to take advantage of a given opportunity. You may be willing to *take* any opportunity, but you should not *search* for any.

- You may be looking for anything, but an employer is not looking for anyone.

- If you are looking for anything, you will never be an employer's someone.

Opportunity Versus Opportunity

- An opportunity is a situation favorable for the attainment of your goal and has an apparent probability of success.

- Not every open position is an opportunity and worth pursuing.

- Acquire the ability to analyze a given situation to determine whether it represents a real opportunity.

- Only pursue real opportunities.

Part Three: Where to Search

Job Boards

- Job boards are websites that post jobs supplied by employers or recruiters; job search engines scour the web and aggregate job listings from job boards and employer websites.

- A job board dependent job search is an ineffective job search.

- You can use job boards as one resource, but you should limit the time you spend and your reliance on these resources.

Recruiters

- Recruiters are not working for you, the job seeker, but for the hiring firm. It is the firm that pays recruiter fees. It is the firm, their client, who they ultimately must satisfy. Recruiters do not earn money by helping you find employment.

Law School Resources

- Law school career services offices are a resource and not a place to unload responsibility.

- Career services staff are guides who help you navigate the job hunt. You cannot expect to have career services staff do the work for you.

The Hidden Job Market

- The hidden job market describes jobs that are not posted online or are otherwise advertised.

- They are not hidden for everyone but only to those outside the community.

- Being a member of the community is an active process that requires acting for the benefit of the community. Being a lawyer does not by itself benefit the community.

Relationships

- You need information, you need valuable information, and you need to find an efficient way to receive such information. The most economical way to receive and spread valuable information is through people.

- If you are not sufficiently connected within the legal community, your job search will suffer from network inequality.

Part Four: How to Search

Online Search

- A job posting is much more than a black or white, apply or don't apply situation. It is one source of information; use it as such to come up with an effective search approach.

- Decide on what you are looking for and create a list of proper keywords to find results.

- Use Boolean strings to help filter search results and avoid an overload of data.

- Once your keywords and Boolean strings produce relevant results, subscribe to email notifications.

- Use LinkedIn, blogs, Twitter, etc., as sources of information about the players in the industry and not just a platform to broadcast your personal brand.

Offline Search

The Productivity Fallacy

- We opt for job boards and applications because it gives us a sense of control over the situation but *feeling* productive does not mean *being* productive.

- Time is a resource and since every resource can be put to alternative uses, every action, choice, or decision has an associated opportunity cost.

- Choose your activity based on what brings the best return on investment.

Building Relationships

- Homophily is the basis of great networking because of our natural tendency to choose people that are similar to us. Begin networking with those closest to you; it is the easiest way to find common ground.

- Homophily is the basis for important networking advice such as:

    - Do your research about the other;

    - Become part;

    - Become active and establish co-presence.

Resume Worthy Activities

- Do not wait for a job to develop your resume.

- Develop your resume while searching for a job by choosing resume worthy activities.

Branding Deeds

- Watch your behavior and act in accordance with how you want to be perceived.

- Branding deeds are the actions that result in an impression of us. Everything we do or do not do brands us.

- Your actions will lead to a judgment about your professional persona, so act accordingly.

Informational Interviews

- An informational interview is a valuable source of information.

- Remember that an informational interview is not a job interview, nor is its purpose to get hired.

- Master the art of skillful questioning.

- The informational interview is only the beginning of the relationship.

Part Five: How to Apply

Applicant Tracking System

- An ATS does not replace human decision making. Instead, it streamlines the hiring process and makes it more efficient.

- The existence of an ATS tells you that you need to honestly assess whether the job and your profile are a true match or just a desperate attempt to get lucky.

Cover Letter

- The strength of our application is proportionate to the amount of information on which it is based.

- The employer does not want to read in the cover letter what she can already see on your resume.

- The employer is not interested in how well this job will fit into your career plans.

- The employer wants to know how what you did in the past will help her in the future. The cover letter creates a bridge between your past and her future.

Resume

- The purpose of your resume is to outline your experience in such a way that it enables the employer to *quickly* and *easily* get a sense of your skill set and professional persona.

- Remember the two R's: Recent and Relevant

Part Six: Nailing the Interview

Before the Interview

- The interview is a conversation between professionals assessing whether they have rapport and whether together they can accomplish the firm's goal.

- Remember "The Cleveland Airport Test." The employer wants to know: do I want to get stuck with that person at the Cleveland Airport?

- Ask yourself: why are you sitting in this room having this conversation at this very moment? If you know why you are having this interview at this firm, for this department and with this person, there is no need to rehearse answers.

- If you have trouble convincing others, you are likely not convinced yourself. Once you are convinced, it is easy to convince others.

During the Interview

- A successful interview depends more on managing yourself than convincing others.

- Remember it is a business conversation not an interrogation.

- The interview can be the beginning of a new professional relationship; enjoy it.

After the Interview

- The interview ends only after the premises have been left behind.

- Follow up with a brief, concrete, and professional note.

Part Seven: Hired

Negotiating an Offer

- Think about all the negotiables that are important to you and always keep the bigger picture in mind.

- Be prepared, be patient, don't play the tough guy, and do not let your emotions get the better of you.
